# HE'S A STUD, SHE'S A SLUT

# HE'S A STUD, SHE'S A SLUT

## AND ⟨49⟩ OTHER DOUBLE STANDARDS EVERY WOMAN SHOULD KNOW

### JESSICA VALENTI

SEAL PRESS

He's a Stud, She's a Slut
and 49 Other Double Standards Every Woman Should Know

Copyright © 2008 by Jessica Valenti

Published by
Seal Press
A Member of Perseus Books Group
1700 Fourth Street
Berkeley, California

Library of Congress Cataloging-in-Publication Data

Valenti, Jessica.
  He's a stud, she's a slut and 49 other double standards every woman should know / by Jessica Valenti.
    p. cm.
  ISBN-13: 978-1-58005-245-0
  ISBN-10: 1-58005-245-2
  1. Women--United States--Public opinion. 2. Men--United States--Public opinion. 3. Stereotypes (Social psychology)--United States. 4. Sexism--United States. 5. Public opinion--United States. I. Title.
  HQ1421.V36 2008
  305.420973--dc22
                                2008004012

10  9  8  7  6  5  4  3  2

Interior design by Megan Cooney
Printed in the United States of America
Distributed by Publishers Group West

To the readers of *Feministing.com,* for inspiring me every day.

# Contents

# INTRODUCTION

**WHEN I WAS IN HIGH SCHOOL,** I had a reputation—a bad one. (You know, a "slutty" one.) I wasn't quite sure how I became seen as the promiscuous girl in school, since I was definitely not getting any more action than my girlfriends. It felt like the reputation—which I really didn't find out about until well into my senior year—had materialized out of nowhere. And I was confused.

Maybe it was because I went to a kind of dorky math and science magnet school where anyone who even talked about sex was labeled sexually active? Perhaps it was because I had so many guy friends that I hung around with? Or maybe it was because I was a little more, ahem, developed than the other gals? I wasn't quite sure.

Looking back, I realize that it could have been any of those things, or nothing. Most likely, it was because I had a bit of a potty mouth (shocking, I know), told dirty jokes, and was a louder, more opinionated girl than some of my peers. I know better now, and realize that labeling girls "sluts" is a pretty common silencing tactic. After all, there's no better way to silence a woman than to call her a whore!

But that was the first sexist double standard I became acutely aware of—one that affected my life and, maybe more important, really pissed me off. I was upset not only that people thought things about me that weren't true, but that the double standard existed in the first place. So fucking what if I *had* slept with every guy in my grade? Why would that make me a bad person? It just seemed so illogical to me, yet it was so accepted. While I didn't consider myself a feminist until college, when I took my first women's studies class, I think it was this sense of just simple unfairness that really got me started down my feminist path.

Because everyday sexism is something that we can all relate to. If you're a feminist or not, a Democrat or Republican, there are certain things that all women recognize—and are pissed off about!

After I wrote my first book, *Full Frontal Feminism,* it was difficult to know what to write next. I got such amazing responses from young women who read the book—women from thirteen to sixty!—I didn't want to let them down with my next one.

One email I got was from a sixteen-year-old Middle Eastern woman living in Michigan who was happy to read something from another young feminist. Another teen, a fourteen-year-old from Mozambique, was pleased that she finally had something that she could use to "get across to my somewhat closed-minded friends for years." The notes that affected me the most, though, were the ones that inspired action. A twenty-one-year-old African American woman from California sent me a message through MySpace about how she faces racism and sexism at work every day: "I thought ideas and feelings like the ones your book and blog have shown me only existed in my hometown of Oakland and S.F. I now want to start a young feminist movement in my community."

I was so touched that these women would take the time to write me, and that the book made an impact on their lives. . . . It was very overwhelming and it still feels like a huge responsibility (one I'm flattered to have!).

And while the notes I got from women came from all different parts of the world, and came from women all across the spectrum in terms of class, race, sexuality, and politics, the one thing they all had in common was that they talked about how sexism affected their everyday lives. Whether it was through sexual harassment or workplace racism or just the struggles they had in school or at home taking care of their kids—it was the day-to-day injustices that women talked about.

So I figured, why not go back to basics? Go back to that place when I hadn't even started to think about feminism yet—but where it was still impossible not to think about and notice day-to-day unfairness and injustice. No matter how anyone feels about feminism, there are certain inequalities and double standards that are impossible to ignore or argue with.

I'm hoping this book will be a fun (but informative!) handbook on those everyday inequities women still face. Because from the boardroom to the bedroom, women are still getting the short end of the stick. Whether it's the sexual double standard that led to me (and so many other women) being labeled a slut, or the work double standard that calls women "bitches" for being good at their job, we still have a long way to go.

This book is for any feminist—or non-feminist!—who is sick of people saying that everything is fine and dandy. This is a book that you'll be able to whip out, whether at school, a bar, or the office, to show the skeptics that sexism is still alive and well—but that there are women out there doing something about it! Think of it as a quick reference guide to everyday sexism. Only funnier.

I hope this book inspires action. I hope that you'll carry it around and use it to battle the sexists in your lives. But most of all, I hope that you leave this book not feeling downtrodden about how pervasive sexism is, but instead energized to do something about it!

That said, I just want to say thanks to all the feminists out there—especially you new feminists!—for doing the hard work, every day, of telling the truth about sexism. I know it's not always easy, but it's changing lives. You all are inspiring.

# 1

#  HE'S A STUD,
## SHE'S A SLUT

**IF YOU HAVE A VAGINA,** chances are someone has called you a slut at least once in your life. There's just no getting around it.

I remember the first time I heard the word "slut"—I was in my fifth-grade science class. A certain little girl (terror) named Eleena had been making my life miserable all year in a way that only mean little girls can. She had turned all of my girlfriends against me, spread rumors and the like. She walked up to me at my desk and said, "You called me a slut." I had absolutely no idea what the word meant. I just sat there, silently. She repeated herself: "You called me a slut, but you're the slut." I don't remember how long after that I found out exactly what "slut" meant, but I knew it had to be terrible and I knew I didn't want to be it.

Naturally, I'd be called a slut many times over later in life—not unlike most girls. I was called a slut when my boobs grew faster than others'. I was called a slut when I had a boyfriend (even though we weren't having sex). I was called a slut when I didn't have a boyfriend and kissed a random boy at a party. I was called a "slut" when I had the nerve to talk about sex. I was called a slut when I wore a bikini on a weekend trip with high school friends. It seems the word "slut" can be applied to any activity that doesn't include knitting, praying, or sitting perfectly still lest any sudden movements be deemed whorish.

Despite the ubiquity of "slut," where you won't hear it is in relation to men. Men can't be sluts. Sure, someone will occasionally call a guy "a dog," but men simply aren't judged like women are when it comes to sexuality. (And if they are, they're judged in a positive way!) Men who have a lot of sexual partners are studs, Casanovas, pimps, and players. Never sluts. In fact, when I just did a Google search for "male sluts," the first result I got was *She Male Sluts DVD!* I know, should have seen that coming. The point is, there isn't even a word—let alone a concept—to signify a male slut.

But it makes sense when you think about what the purpose of the word "slut" is: controlling women through shame and humiliation. Women's bodies are *always* the ones that are being vied over for control—whether it's rape, reproductive rights, or violence against women, it's our bodies that are the battleground, not men's.

And if you don't think it's about control, consider this little bit of weirdness. The most recent incarnation of the sexual double standard being played out in a seriously creepy way is through Purity Balls. These promlike events basically have fathers take their daughters to a big fancy dance where they promise their daddy their virginity. Likewise, the father promises to be the "keeper" of his daughter's virginity until he decides to give it to her future husband. Where are the Purity Balls for men, you ask? Oh, they're there, but they're about controlling women too! Called Integrity Balls, these events focus on men not having sex because they'd be defiling someone else's "future wife"! Not because men need to be pure or be virgins—but because they need to make sure *women* are virgins. Unbelievable, really.

Outside of the feminist implications of the sexual double standard, the slut/stud conundrum has always been my favorite because it just makes no sense logically. Why is a woman less of a person, or (my favorite) "dirty," because she has sex? (Heterosexual sex, that is; somehow lesbian sex isn't "real.") Does a penis have some bizarre dirty-making power that I'm unaware of? Every time I have sex, do I lose a little bit of my moral compass? "Sorry to mug you, Grandma, but I had sex twice this week!"

And let's face it—the slut stigma isn't just dangerous to our "reputations" or to some weird-ass notion of purity. How many times has a rape been discounted because a woman was deemed a slut? How many times are women called whores while their partners beat them? How often are women's sexual histories used against them in workplace harassment cases? The sexual double standard is a lot more dangerous than we'd like to think.

# So... *what to do?*

First and foremost, stop calling other women sluts! It doesn't behoove us to bash each other, gals. And speak out when you hear men do the same. I'll never forget in college overhearing a conversation that my boyfriend's roommates were having. They both had slept with the same girl over the course of the year—they called her a whore and made a joke about her vagina being "loose." I asked them why she was the bad person in this scenario—after all, they had had casual sex with her, too. They couldn't provide an answer, but that didn't stop them from continuing to laugh. I always regretted not saying anything more. Outside of calling ourselves and others out on perpetuating the double standard, it's a hard battle. But I think if we recognize the hypocrisy of the stud/slut nonsense when we see it—whether it's in an anti-choice law or a movie that makes women who have sex look like deviants—we're on the right road.

(Random true story: When I was in my early twenties, I was watching a documentary on anorexia and saw my childhood tormentor, Eleena, talking about her terrible eating disorder and how she cut herself as a teen. Just something to remember when you think back on the kids who were cruel to you—they were in pain, too.)

# ♠ HE'S CHILL,
## SHE'S ON THE PILL

**IN MY SEX-HAVING LIFETIME,** I've been on the Pill, used the NuvaRing, condoms, and female condoms, and considered getting an IUD just so I wouldn't have to worry about birth control for another five years or so. I've taken emergency contraception. The job of being responsible, at the end of the day, has always lain with me. Because I'm a woman. It's our responsibility to have safe sex: birth control pills, diaphragms, spermicides—shit, we even have to convince men to wear condoms! I say it's crap.

There's no doubt that women will always have a disproportionate amount of responsibility when it comes to sex, because we're the ones who get pregnant—and if we do get pregnant it's going to be up to us to decide what to do about it. But the way that birth control is automatically considered a woman's domain is just irksome, not only from a theoretical feminist perspective—why should it only be up to us!?—but also from a practical one.

Because being the responsible party in a sexual relationship doesn't come without costs. Birth control has always cost me money, but recently I'm spending over $50 a month (I don't have health insurance) to make sure I don't get knocked up. And I know I'm not the only one who is breaking the bank.

# 2

I used to long for my college days, when being on the Pill would only cost me a few dollars a month. But those days are long gone, and young women today are getting totally screwed. Birth control prices on college campuses are literally doubling and tripling. (But not condoms, of course—just the kind that the ladies use.) Drug companies that used to sell colleges contraceptives at a discount—which is why you could get a $50 pack of pills for $12—have stopped offering the discount. And women are pissed, rightfully. The best quote I heard about this increase in price came from a twenty-two-year-old at the University of Iowa who said, "This is the one thing that many females on campus are getting from student health. . . . It felt like we were a target." [1] Ya think?

And the cost of bearing birth control responsibility isn't just monetary. Birth control has long been used against certain women—women of color, immigrants, and low-income women—as a way to control them. There are groups that put up billboards in low-income, minority communities urging women to get sterilized for cash (seriously), and a long history of sterilizing women because only certain (white) women having babies is considered desirable.

Unfortunately, it's not only the onus of being protected that's on women, it's also the stigma attached to having sex. Men can buy condoms without getting a lecture or a problem—but women who go to the pharmacy for birth control are often refused or asked about their marital status. Can you even *imagine* that happening to a man? And when was the last time you saw conservative groups up in arms about condoms being available in schools? Hell no. Because they couldn't give a shit about whether guys have sex or not. But allowing women to take control of their reproductive destinies? No way. There have been all sorts of protests just in the last year over birth control pills and patches being made available to young women. So not only is it up to us to make sure we're protected—we have to jump through all sorts of hoops to make it happen!

So what about the men? You would think that men would be eager to take on extra responsibility—having control over your reproductive future is always a good thing, after all. A common anti-feminist argument against child support, for example, is that women constantly trick men into getting them pregnant (sure they do). Guess what, guys—if you used a condom every time you had sex, and took some responsibility for your sex life, you would never have to worry about something like that.

When I've asked folks (friends, foes, and even feminists) about the birth control disparity, I've heard countless times that it's not *their* fault that all of the contraceptive options are available to women. But recent studies show that the lack of a male birth control pill, which has been reported to be on its way for years now, isn't because of science holdups—it's societal obstacles. The man who originally developed the male pill, Carl Djerassi, says they stopped working on it because men just wouldn't use it: "It would be possible to make a male pill today. We know how hormones work and we could use the same principles that are used to make the female [pill]....The problem is that men are afraid to lose their virility. Even if taking a pill carries only a remote chance of impotence, they won't take the chance." (Ri-ight. Because it's not like women undertake any health risks at all using countless levels of hormones, things stuck up our chocha, and the like.)

# So... what to do?

If you're straight and sexually active, make sure that your partner is taking on as much responsibility as you are. Use condoms. Split the costs of all your birth control—after all, he's benefiting from it, too! At the end of the day, the birth control double standard exists for one reason—sexism. The idea behind the reality of fewer BC options for men is that sex and reproduction are all about women. We can't let them be.

# ♦ HE'S ROUGH,
## SHE'S DAINTY

# 3

**WHEN I WAS SIX YEARS OLD,** I had a play kitchen set—it was tin and looked super real. I also had a tea set and a shit ton of dolls. But, thanks to my hippie parents, I also had a Thundercats glowing sword, toy robots, and multiple racing car sets (those were my favorite). And while I was acutely aware that there were "boys' toys" and "girls' toys," I remember always appreciating my parents telling me that girls could play with boys' toys and vice versa. (Especially because I took some shit from schoolmates due to my penchant for swords and robots.) I never would have thought that twenty-three years later children would have the same kind of gendered toys that I grew up with.

You really don't need to look much further than the nonsense directed at our children to see a ton of double standards at play, not to mention the way that sexist socialization starts early.

Take toys, for example. You can still find the "girls'" aisle in a toy store just by looking for the blinding pink that adorns everything. Feministing.com blogger Vanessa (and my sis) took a look at the toys sold in superstore Target and found some predictable, though no less nauseating, trends: Girls' toys are supposed to "make her sweet dreams come true," with featured sections, the first being "Kitchen and Play Food," along with "Dolls and Accessories" and "Horse Play Sets." Boys' toys "let his imagination run wild" with "Cars, Trucks, and Trains,"

"Building and Construction," "Tech Toys and Kids' Electronics," "Vehicles and Radio Control," and "Science."

But it's not just the pink-is-for-girls, blue-is-for-boys trend that's problematic. It's what these toys are, and what they're telling our kids from a very early age.

Take the Fashion Fever Shopping Boutique, a Barbie toy that has a pink credit card swiper and credit card so that little girls can "buy" outfits for their dolls. The television commercial for the toy features a little girl saying, "And you never run out of money!" (You know, just like in real life. Sigh.) Creating good little consumers one toy at a time! Never mind that young women in the United States are deeper in credit card debt than perhaps any other group in the country.[1]

Or Playskool's new Rose Petal Cottage—the tagline for this girls' playhouse is "Where dreams have room to grow." That is, of course, assuming your daughter's dreams consist of baking muffins, rocking a cradle, and doing laundry. The commercial for the toy is totally disturbing, with lyrics from the Rose Petal Cottage song saying: "I love when my laundry gets so clean / Taking care of my home is a dream, dream, dream!" If that's not bad enough, when the little girl in the commercial puts clothes in her laundry machine, the narrator notes the cottage is a place "she can entertain her imagination"! Girls' imaginations should consist of laundry and baking. Awesome. Compare that with Tonka, whose new commercials claim that "boys are different" and that their trucks are built "Tonka tough," and I think you'll see what I'm getting at. Not to mention the racism built into so many toys, especially for girls. Most dolls sold are white and blond, and those that are supposed to be "ethnic" have overwhelmingly Caucasian features.

And if toys aren't telling little girls that they should grow up to be happy homemakers, they're telling them to be sexual. Seriously. It was just 2006 when Target took shit for selling padded bras for girls as young as six. A spokesperson from Bratz, who makes the "bralettes," said "the idea of the padding is for girls to be discreet as they develop." Um, last time I checked, six-year-olds had nothing to be discreet about. British superstore Tesco even got called out for selling toy stripper poles in the children's toy section. The kit is advertised on its site as saying, "Unleash the sex kitten inside.... Simply extend the Peekaboo pole inside the tube, slip on the sexy tunes, and away you go!" Charming.

Then there's clothing. If you've ever shopped for a little girl—especially a baby girl—I challenge you to find something that (a) isn't pink and (b) doesn't say something like "princess" or "diva" or "drama queen." Not possible. Jane Roper, on her blog, Baby Squared, says of the clothing conundrum: "I guess some people find it funny. Like: Ha, ha—an innocent baby girl can't be a spoiled pain in the ass! So it's funny to call her one! Because, really, she won't be a spoiled pain in the ass until she's at least twelve! And if she is one then, that's fine! Because that's just what it means to be an empowered young woman in America today! Getting what you want—whether it's shoes or clothes or an iPod or a chihuahua or your own reality show or whatever. God bless America! Ha, ha, ha! Princess! How cute!" And how sad. And I haven't even touched on child beauty pageants, television shows, and a ton of other stuff directed at children.

# So... what to do?

Don't buy your kids sexist toys! Which I know isn't easy, I assure you. Or if you *must* buy the goddamn Rose Petal Cottage, get some Tonka trucks too. (Though it's probably better that you don't support toy companies that rely on sexism to sell their products!) If you're looking for cool, not-all-white dolls, check out Karito Kids, which features girls from all over the world. (Think American Girl but cooler and international.) Go to parent blogs dedicated to anti-sexism and anti-racism for ideas. And for goodness' sake, stay away from toy credit cards.

# 4  ♀ HE'S A HERO, ♀ SHE'S A DAMSEL

**DESPITE MY PARENTS' PROTESTATIONS,** I must admit that I'm far from perfect. I'm loud and sarcastic, and when I'm pissed I can be a cold bitch. Like all people, I have my flaws. Which is why I've never, ever wanted a guy to put me on a pedestal—if you're on a pedestal, you have a long way to fall. And no one can live up to the expectations that some folks—in fact, a lot of folks—have for women. That we're virgins, Madonnas, mothers, little girls, perfect angels to be protected. Naturally, viewing women this way sets up a very dangerous dynamic—because no one is perfect, and when women transgress, they get punished. (You don't have to look much further than the virgin/whore complex to figure that out.)

And while the whole woman-on-a-pedestal thing is often shrouded in ideas about romance, it's anything but. Because notions of pedestals and chivalry operate under the assumption that women are inferior. While holding women up to high standards may not immediately seem like it's degrading—after all, right now the idea of girls being "princesses" and "treated like queens" is all the rage (just watch *Bridezillas*)—what it's actually doing is saying that women are like children, not fully formed people. We have to be protected. We have to be coddled. We have to be treated with kid gloves. Sorry, but my idea of romance isn't being babied.

Now, when people think "chivalry," they think of men opening doors for women, throwing their jackets over puddles, and paying for dinners. All admittedly nice things, save the jacket throwing—that just seems nuts, given the price of outerwear these days. But this is how they get you. Doing things like opening doors for people is *polite*. I would hope one would do as much for anyone if they got to the door first. Chivalry is something completely different. Chivalry is the idea that men should be doing something for women for one of two reasons: They think women aren't capable of doing things for themselves; they think that doing things like opening doors should get them laid. Again, I think doing nice things for people, whether you're dating them or not, is fantastic. I love it when my significant other does shit for me (now, whether this is because I'm slightly lazy, I don't know). But we should draw a distinction.

One of my favorite examples of chivalry gone wild is from a column in a college paper that my friend and fellow feminist blogger Jill Filopovic wrote about. Basically, this male student is complaining that chivalry is dead because women had the audacity to do things for themselves: "And so emerged a group of warrior princesses affectionately referred to as Feminazis; lean, mean, emasculating machines in power suits who proved to the world that women are intelligent, strong, capable, and incredibly frightening." You have to love a guy who thinks capable women are "frightening." Jill's response to this is spot on:

> There's a difference between being chivalrous and being nice or polite. Opening a door for someone because you got to the door first is both nice and polite; making a huge production of opening a door for a woman in the hopes that she'll see

what a chivalrous dude you are and fuck you (and then getting all pissy when she doesn't respond how you want her to) is not polite or nice. And that's the thing with chivalry: It always demands something in return. If you're being nice to me because you like me and you're the kind of person who is nice to people you like, then that's great. If you're being nice to me because you're hoping to get something out of it, or if you think you're entitled to sex or a relationship with me because you were nice and "chivalrous," you can go fuck yourself. See how that works?

Love it. And frankly, when you take a look at the people who are pushing old-school notions of chivalry and romance, you may think twice before letting a dude pick up the check. Most often, it's conservatives you'll hear arguing that chivalry is dead. (And that feminists killed it, of course.) These are folks who have a specific agenda in mind—mostly one that involves getting women back in the kitchen. For real.

Conservative women's group the Independent Women's Forum, for example, has a campaign called "Take Back the Date," where they try to counter what they call "hookup culture" by promoting old-school dating practices—like bringing flowers, boys asking girls out and never vice versa, and so on. Doesn't really sound terrible, right? Well, the *other* part of "Taking Back the Date" is protesting feminists on campus and any college performances of *The Vagina Monologues*. (Because talking about vaginas is counter to romance, apparently.) They see promoting chivalry as an easy way to promote other traditional gender roles.

Chivalry is also used as an excuse to glorify the "good old days" when men were men and women were doormats. In fact, *New York Times* columnist David Brooks once wrote that the reason rape still exists is that chivalry is no longer around. (As if women didn't get raped in the good old days. Uh-huh.) So seriously, let's not romanticize something that's not necessarily all that great.

So... what to do?

I'm not going to lie: I'm not going to stop letting guys open doors for me, and I'll probably still like it when someone offers to help me put my jacket on. But I'm not going to *expect* it from men. Similarly, I would hope that men—upon doing random nice things—wouldn't expect anything in return. And when it comes to the dangers of being on a pedestal, just don't go there.

# 5

# HE'S METROSEXUAL,
## SHE'S ANOREXIC

**UNREALISTIC BEAUTY STANDARDS** are one of those feminist topics that you have to love—because no one in their right mind can argue that they don't exist. We see images of unattainable beauty norms everywhere—in magazines, television, advertisements, movies, you name it. All touting the same image of what's supposed to be an attractive woman: white, thin, blond (usually), big boobs, the whole package. And sure, men have beauty standards to live up to as well. But not nearly on the same level as women. Attractiveness standards for men tell them to be big, strong, to take up space. Our beauty standards tell us to shrink, be weak, take up as little space as possible.

Then, of course, men's beauty standards tend to end *above* the waist. For women, it's no longer good enough to be emaciated, tanned, siliconed, shaved, and just generally trussed up. Now we have to make sure that every inch of us—even the naughty bits—is equally "beautiful."

Seriously, where are men's penis-beauty standards? Yes, men get circumcised, but the new labiaplasty trend—where women have their vaginas tightened and lips shortened in order to have prettier pussies (whatever that means)—goes above and beyond.

Labiaplasty—or "vaginal rejuvenation surgery"—is one of the fastest-growing plastic surgeries out there, despite being dangerous, painful, and potentially damaging to your ability to have pleasurable sex. The American College of Obstetricians and Gynecologists released a public warning against the surgery, noting that potential risks include "infection, scarring, nerve damage, and loss of sensation."[1] Good times.

So why would women line up to get the surgery? Because these charming docs, along with the porn industry and lad-mad culture, are telling women that their normal vaginas are ugly and vile the way they are. And isn't that more important than your future relationship with orgasms?

Now, the same folks who brought you your newfound vaginal insecurities are pushing surgery packages with empowering-sounding names like "Wonder Woman Makeover," which includes "several vaginal procedures, breast implants and a breast lift, abdominal liposuction, and a 'Brazilian butt augmentation.'" Where are the Superman Makeovers, you ask? Sorry, no such thing.

There are also no "Daddy Makeovers" to compare to the new trend of "Mommy Makeovers," either—this is when moms who have just had kids get surgery to "fix" their postpartum bodies. (I can see the male version now. Dads, get rid of that beer gut! Your wife will love your new toned physique!)

And it's not just the usual suspects of body parts when it comes to beauty standards. Another new and improved way to maim—I mean 'improve'—yourself: Now you can fit into those designer shoes by cutting off your toes. Or shortening them. For real—people are actually doing this. Dr Ali Sadrieh, a podiatrist from California, says, "Toes are the new nose." Now, I like heels as much as the next gal, but generally I look for shoes to fit my feet—not feet to fit my shoes. Just saying.

The old standard of weight is still around as well, naturally. But now instead of just being thin, we have to be dying. Literally. The covers of celebrity weeklies are covered with anorexic starlets, their bones jutting out from sagging skin and oversize sunglasses. Of course, the headlines feign concern ("Brad to Angelina: You have to eat!"; "Nicole's struggle with weight"), but they're glamorizing the disease simply by having these women on the cover. Being a sickly-thin celeb is a surefire way to rev up your career (second to having a baby, of course).

The common theme here? Beauty standards for women are more extreme than ever. (There's even the reality show *Extreme Makeover* to prove it!) Pop culture has everything revved up—we can't have normal sex, it has to be porn sex. We can't have normal vaginas, they have to be teeny, tiny, hairless vaginas. We can't be skinny, we have to be anorexic. It's just all too much to live up to.

 **So... what to do?**

Don't believe the hype. (Yes, I am a Public Enemy fan.) And for the love of all things natural, don't get surgery—it's just bad news. And when it comes to the images that are shoved in our faces day after day, be a critical thinker. (Easier said than done, sometimes.) To steal some advice from my girl Courtney Martin, author of *Perfect Girls, Starving Daughters*, who wrote a great piece on loving your body for Feministing:

> "Never diet. Never ever. It is a $31 billion industry that fails 95 percent of the time. That's just stupid. Don't spend money on products made by companies that make you feel inadequate. Duh. Redefine your notion of success to include your own wellness—including joy, fulfillment, resilience, and self-love."

Yeah, she's a little hippie-ish, but she's a smart lady. Listen to her. Plus, I love hippies.

# 6

# ♀ HE'S "LUCKY,"
## SHE'S LOLITA

**WHEN I WAS SIXTEEN YEARS OLD** I met the hottest guy ever. He was six-three, muscular, and had a (swoon) tattoo on his arm. He was also twenty. Not the ideal age, I admit, but Jason and I had a great time together. Looking back, though, I can say with certainty that I was much more mature than he was at the time. (I was taking Organic Chemistry; he was applying to be on *The Real World*. Just saying.) We had a decent yearlong relationship that ended when his modeling/acting career didn't take off (don't laugh) and he moved back home to upstate New York. A fairly normal romance? Actually, no. Under New York state law, Jason could have been arrested for statutory rape, even though our relationship was consensual.

Fucked up for him? Absolutely. Men are prosecuted every year for statutory rape despite being in consensual relationships. (That isn't to say I think there shouldn't be consent laws *at all*, but clearly something needs to change when innocent men are going to jail and young women are being told they don't have the right to have sex.)

While—like a lot of sexism—this affects both men and women, the double standards in consent laws are mired in misogyny. Teenage girls who have sex can be either victims or whores. That's it. We're either poor little virginal things who were taken advantage of or hot-to-trot vixens who seduced our way through high school. (Sounds like a Lifetime movie already!) Men, on the other hand, are able to have sex whenever they want. You know, because unlike women, they *like* sex. (Sigh.) No one questions if they were taken advantage of. I mean, even in recent cases in the media where older female teachers had sex with young male students, there were comments about how "lucky" the boy was.

This teen-sex double standard is based on the antiquated—and false—notion that women don't like sex. Or at least we shouldn't.

The problem for women with consent laws, and really anything to do with ideas surrounding teen sex, is that women are assumed to be victims simply because of our age. The logic is that we don't have the wherewithal to make up our own minds about sex. Now, do all girls have the emotional maturity to have a sexual relationship? Of course not. But plenty of teenagers do—unfortunately, a lot of folks can't handle that. To be clear, I'm not talking about a fifteen-year-old dating some creepy thirty-year-old. There's no doubt that with certain age differences (whether it's men or women who are older) there's a power dynamic that makes real informed consent almost impossible.

But are we so invested in the idea of teen girls as little virginal angels that we can't be honest about their sexual desires? Young women can choose to have sex. They can choose not to. For too many people, that's just too much freedom for young women to have.

And when we have laws that are based on the idea that young women couldn't possibly want to have sex, we have an issue. Because under this framework, when it's clear that young women *are* choosing to have sex, it means there's something wrong with them—they must be whores.

Of course, there is a way out of the virgin/whore trap—marriage. The virgin/whore complex is hard at work on this one! If you're married, you can have any kind of sex you want! Shit, if you're thirteen years old and married in Kansas, your sex is legal. If you're sixteen years old but unmarried, not so much. Which, of course, is the real point of all this nonsense: keeping young women pure (whatever that means). If we're married, no matter what our age or maturity level, somehow our sex is sanctioned. So, at the end of the day, these laws and ideas about teen girls and sex aren't about keeping us safe. They aren't about protecting young women or caring about their well-being. They're about making sure girls remain chaste.

# So... what to do?

Let's start by not judging young women on what their sexual lives are like. Let's not assume young women shouldn't want to have sex, and that young men should. And instead of assuming that a young woman who is sexually active is somehow a victim or a slut, let's make no assumptions. At all. And let's start talking about how to really talk to young women about sex. We're so caught up in the idea that teen girls are victims or vixens that we don't prepare them to be something in between—informed, mature, aware young women. It's time to start doing just that.

# HE'S A BACHELOR,
## SHE'S A SPINSTER

**THERE'S SOMETHING HOT ABOUT SINGLE MEN.** They're bachelors, with cool apartments and the freedom to do whatever they want without judgment. Sure, they may catch occasional shit from their mother about "finding the right girl," but for the most part they're respected. Single women, on the other hand—especially single women who have the gall to be over thirty—we're old maids. Spinsters. Desperate to be Bridezillas and moms. There's no such thing as a happy single woman. We're all just wives-in-training or crazy cat ladies.

There's something about unmarried women that society just doesn't like. That's why the media is constantly telling us how miserable single women are. For example, *The Today Show* ran a segment about single working women where an editor for *Marie Claire* called women who don't get married and have kids "fembots." You know, 'cause we must be robotic and frigid if we want careers before we have a family. The editor actually went so far as to call women who care a lot about their careers "emotionally unavailable." But painting women who don't get married as vicious career women or sad old spinsters is nothing new.

As I wrote in an essay for *Single State of the Union*,[1] the media likes to portray single women as caricatures. If we're young and "sexy," we're "office piranhas" trying to steal married men. If we're older, either we're desperate or we're "cougars." And the bad science studies come out in force when it comes to single gals: The new trend is reporting that women won't get married if they're too successful, too educated, or too old—as in over twenty-five.

The most annoying thing about these stereotypes and "studies" is that they assume that all women want to get married and that all women are straight! (Lesbian women just don't exist when it comes to the media these days.)

The scary truth (at least, what society sees as scary) is that women may be better off *not* getting married. One of my favorite writers, Natalie Angier, wrote a piece for *The New York Times* a while back about how marriage really benefits men more than it does women (despite the media-created frenzy about women just dying to get married and men wanting to put it off):

> In 1972 ... Jesse Bernard wrote a highly influential book called *The Future of Marriage* in which she argued that wedding bells sounded the death knell to a woman's well-being. Ms. Bernard presented data indicating that while married men scored higher than single men on measures of mental health like depression, severe neurotic symptoms, and phobic tendencies, the opposite applied for women.[2]

Angier points out that this isn't the case for all women, obviously, and that, depending on the kind of partner someone has, everyone's situation is different. But it does give me pause. As does the study that showed that married women do a ton more housework than men—there's even a marked difference when you live with a man as opposed to being married. (Living together there's less housework; married you do more—whatever.)

Now, this certainly isn't a diatribe against marriage—I'd like to get married one day. But making marriage seem like the end goal for all women and the Best Thing Ever just isn't honest.

And if marriage is so amazing and great, why would conservatives need all of these initiatives, organizations, and legislation to push women to get hitched? Wouldn't the joy of being a wife be enough? Apparently not.

Conservatives are recognizing that more and more women aren't rushing to the altar—plenty of couples are cohabiting, and people are waiting until they're a bit older to get hitched. Then, of course, there's the divorce rate. So, because they're so tied to the idea of marriage holding together traditional gender roles, they're taking action. There's even a lawmaker in Idaho who is doing his best to try to create legislation that would essentially trap women in marriage and push them to stay at home instead of working in the public sphere: Chairman of the Idaho House of Representatives' Family Task Force, Rep. Steven Thayn, is trying to repeal no-fault divorce laws and convening task forces to figure out ways to encourage mothers to stay home with their children. Funny that initiatives like these never target men. And notice that these groups, who seem to just love marriage, aren't so concerned with making same-sex marriage legal. Imagine that.

It's all about getting single women married, because there's a belief that married women will mean traditional women. And that's scary.

# So... *what to do?*

Get married, by all means. But don't do it because you think you need to in order to be a full person, or because the media is breathing down your neck with bullshit statistics about successful, smart women missing out on the hubby train because they had the nerve to care about their own single lives. Start referring to yourself as a bachelorette and enjoy your single life! (And while you're at it, make sure you're fighting for same-sex marriage, because what good is doing something that's being used to discriminate against so many people?)

# 8

# ♀HE CAN BE A BEAST,
## SHE MUST BE A BEAUTY

**LOOKING AT MOVIES AND TELEVISION THESE DAYS,** it would seem that every dumpy, immature guy gets an absurdly hot, successful girlfriend issued to him at birth. Whether they're featured in *The King of Queens* or *Knocked Up,* beautiful, accomplished women just seem to be attracted to schlubs.

Now, don't get me wrong—I've dated my fair share of schlubs. There was the semi-alcoholic, slightly overweight goth boy who deserted me in the middle of Bumblefuck, Queens, one night after a couple too many drinks. Or the Brooklyn hipster with an eczema problem who had a penchant for emailing women in the Craigslist "casual encounters" section. But hey, we're all allowed some dating snafus. And I didn't *marry* the schlubs. Because that would be crazy—not to mention unrealistic. And, yes, I realize that television isn't the best place to look for the non-crazy these days, but seriously—the Marge/Homer marriage model has got to go.

Because while some would say that this fictitious relationship model makes men look like bumbling idiots, it makes women look even worse. After all, they're the ones who stay with said schlubs despite knowing better. It's incredibly insulting.

And it's not just the looks disparity—this isn't all about eye rolling at the seemingly never-ending depictions of plain men getting gorgeous women (though a little eye rolling is probably warranted). It's about the fact that men in the media are paired up with women whom, let's face it, they probably don't deserve. And while the "morals" of so many of these stories, like *Knocked Up,* show the protagonists growing up and ceasing to be complete assholes, the message seems to be that men only have to aim to be basically decent human beings to snag a beautiful, successful woman. That if they can just be, well, normal—any woman will jump to be with them.

Now, *Knocked Up* may not be the very best example for me to use, because I have a bit of a thing for Seth Rogan. Call me crazy—I like the chub. But it *is* pretty interesting. The whole premise of the movie is that this slacker dude can score a relationship with a hot, successful woman by getting her pregnant (so she'll stick around long enough to see that he's a nice guy) and acting halfway decent. It's similar with television shows featuring the bumbling hubby—women find ineptitude *charming,* didn't ya know?

Now, if this were just a silly television trend, I probably wouldn't be all that upset over it. But the *idea* behind the silly trend is making for some serious entitlement issues. All of a sudden, the dating climate is chock-full of men who think that they need to just sit back, relax, and the universe will deliver them a supermodel.

A guy friend of mine (who shall remain nameless) once had a long conversation with me bemoaning the fact that he couldn't find a girlfriend. He's a better-than-average-looking guy, smart and funny—

so I couldn't understand it either. Until he started explaining the kind of girl he was looking for, and the girls he had turned down. You see, my friend was only interested in dating a gal who looked, well, like a *Playboy* model. And I'm sad to say he's not the only friend I have who thinks this way. Women whom they date are not partners as much as they are status symbols—so being with a ridiculously hot woman was a priority over smarts, kindness, humor, anything. This isn't to say I think people should just disregard attractiveness in dating—obviously, we all have our types. But when young men think that they're entitled to have a super-hot model girlfriend, there's kind of a problem. And frankly, a lot of young men are going to find themselves highly disappointed in the relationships they have (or never get) if they think the only women worth having are those just there to be arm candy.

Not to mention what this does to women. It reinforces the idea that we're trophies and that we don't really need someone who is our equal (or even someone who is smart and charming)—just anyone who doesn't act like a *total* asshole is fine.

# So... what to do?

Don't date schlubs. Just kidding. I don't think the loser-gets-hottie model is about to go anywhere anytime soon. But I do think we can do something about it in our own lives. For example, call dudes out on their sense of entitlement. I wish I had said something to my guy friend . . . maybe something along the lines of, "Shut the fuck up about girls with big boobs and waxed vajayjays for a second and focus on what's really important." But I digress. It's time to point out the ridiculousness of this double standard—whenever we can. And, as always, don't believe the hype.

# 9

# HE'S A HIPSTER,
## SHE'S A HO

**THERE'S NO DOUBT THAT WOMEN ARE EXPECTED** to look a certain way—we all know what the unrealistic beauty standards are in this country (skinny, white, big breasts, and so on). But it's not just our bodies that are privy to sexism—the way we present them is as well.

Women are never, ever supposed to dress shlumpy or seem unkempt—but on the other hand, we're chastised if we dress too "sexy."

When I was promoting my first book, I went on Comedy Central's *The Colbert Report*. I was extremely excited and nervous, especially about what to wear. I knew that because I was a feminist, I would be judged more harshly for the way I looked. I decided to go for a businesslike outfit: a white button-down shirt, blue knee-length skirt, and pumps. Super simple. After the show aired, one of the first emails I got was from a guy who told me I was obviously "trying to show off [my] legs" by wearing a skirt and heels, and that I was "flaunting" my sexuality. It wasn't the only email I got to that effect. It's amazing, really. Women are seen so much as public property, as objects to look at and judge, that people actually think it's appropriate to go out of their way to comment on women's appearance. They think it's their right.

JESSICA VALENTI

For example, Southwest Airlines harassed two women (in separate instances) for dressing "inappropriately." In the first incident, a young woman was told by a flight attendant that her outfit was too revealing—and that she would have to change or miss her flight. Was she sporting a bikini? A bra and hot pants? Nope—just a sweater and miniskirt. Another woman just weeks later was told to cover up with a blanket—she was wearing a tank top. Just a side note: When was the last time that a guy with a beer belly hanging out of his shirt was reprimanded?

The only thing I saw that these two women flying Southwest had in common (in the pictures) was that they were both very pretty by conventional beauty standards, and they were both well endowed in the boobie department. Now, as someone with not-small breasts, nothing pisses me off more than when someone assumes my outfit is too "sexy" just because of said breasts' presence. We can't help it! And even if these women *were* dressing in a deliberately sexy way—so what? They're only doing what society basically demands of them. And, let's be honest, if we don't dress to impress, we still have to put up with bullshit.

Just take Darlene Jespersen, a bartender in Reno, Nevada, who sued her boss for trying to force her to wear makeup. She had worked at Harrah's casino for twenty-one years, and she said she just didn't want to wear powder, blush, mascara, and lipstick—which were part of the dress code for the female employees at the bar. Seems pretty reasonable to me. But she actually lost her case; a court of appeals ruled that the casino *can* force women to wear makeup. So if we dress up we're whores, and if we don't we're sloppy. There's no winning for women.

Then, of course, we also have to deal with the maintenance double standards. Women—if we don't want to be accused of being ugly or lazy—have to maintain a certain level of contrived "prettiness." This requires makeup, body-hair removal, tanning beds, manicures and pedicures, dieting, push-up bras, uncomfortable shoes, uncomfortable clothes . . . the list goes on and on. All so we can't be accused of not at least *trying* to be pretty.

Men, on the other hand, barely need to run a comb through their hair to be considered put together! And while there's the whole new "metrosexual" trend—guys who get waxed and tanned, get facials, and buy more hair gel than their girlfriends—they're more mocked for being feminine than considered hot and manly.

And, like so many other seemingly superficial double standards, the clothing conundrum has a lot more at stake than a woman's ability to wear a skirt without getting crap from a flight attendant or having to deal with waxing her cooter on a regular basis. Women are still routinely blamed for their own rapes and sexual assaults based on what they were wearing. An Amnesty International study found that 26 percent of people think that if a woman wears sexy clothes, she's partly to blame if she gets raped—and women's outfits are still brought up as relevant in rape cases. It's vile.

# So... what to do?

One thing is for sure—don't stop dressing the way you like. Whether it's heels and lipstick or beat-up jeans and sneakers that do it for you, just wear it and don't let anyone give you shit for it. And if you hear someone making comments about women's clothing, speak up. Don't let sexism go unnoticed—even if it is "just" about fashion.

# 10

# HE'S GONNA BE A SUCCESS,
## SHE'S GONNA BE A STAY-AT-HOME MOM

**WHEN I WAS IN HIGH SCHOOL,** my boyfriend tried to convince me that men were "naturally" inclined to cheat. Men were supposed to be polygamous, and women were hardwired to be monogamous, he reasoned. It was scientific and stuff. (I know, be wary of teenage boys arguing that philandering is just a male instinct.)

When it comes to the battle of the sexes, bad science always seems to be caught in the middle. Conservative groups use it to try to argue that women belong in the kitchen, antifeminists use it to claim victory in their warped logic, and the media eats it up and uses it to spread sexist misinformation. Why? Because sexism sells. Caryl Rivers, author of *Selling Anxiety: How the News Media Scare Women*, notes that the most popular stories in *The New York Times* in the last few years have all been about bad science studies claiming that men won't marry smart women, and that highly educated women all want to be housewives.

It's all part of the backlash against feminism. Women are doing well, so best to try to convince them that they're miserable because of it.

(Susan Faludi's *Backlash* was all about this phenomenon in the '80s.) Or that women are really meant for traditional "ladylike" things—like ironing and other fascinating chores—and that the urge they felt to work in the public sphere was just a nasty aftereffect of evil feminism. After all, it's certainly not a coincidence that some of the most popular bad science topics either reinforce traditional gender roles or shame women who dare to live beyond them.

Like the one from the University of California, Santa Barbara, that reported women are better at grocery shopping. Or another that said women are naturally suited to housework. (You know, because a skill for vacuuming goes hand in hand with having a vagina.) There was even a study in the U.K. that got a lot of media play that reported moms who work outside the home end up having overweight children. "Working moms have obese kids!" You sensing a bit of a trend here?

The backlash is as strong as ever.

And if it isn't the reinforcing of gender roles, it's the plain old women-are-stupid studies. If we listened to these junk science reports, we'd believe that women are worse at science, math, map reading, logical reasoning, spatial abilities, driving, networking, leadership skills . . . even making jokes.

Other favorite "studies" of mine include these oh-so-compelling ideas:

* Housework cuts women's risk of breast cancer.
* Men chase beauty, women, and money, when picking a mate.
* Hook-up culture is destroying young women.
* Smart and educated women can't find husbands.

* Divorced women are more likely to be mentally ill.

* Men are smarter than women (seriously, this was a study that someone got frigging funding for).

Sometimes I even think that these dudes make stuff up just to make themselves feel better. For example, in perhaps the best-titled article ever, "Crying Over Spilled Semen," *Psychology Today* reported on a study that basically said women are *addicted* to semen. Amazing:

> The finding that women who do not use condoms during sex are less depressed and less likely to attempt suicide than are women who have sex with condoms and women who are not sexually active leads one researcher to conclude that semen contains powerful—and potentially addictive—mood-altering chemicals.

The study's author also said that he's planning on examining whether "semen withdrawal" places women at an increased risk for depression.

The one thing all of these "studies" have in common? They're just not true. Or they've been debunked. Or the media that report on them exaggerate the stuff they think is the juiciest.

Of course, there *are* some studies I can get behind. Like the 2007 one from Rutgers University in New Jersey that said feminists have better relationships and sex.[1] So there.

# So... what to do?

I think we've all had it up to here with sexism that gets the support of the "scientific" community and the media. Now, there's no way for us to completely change the studies that are done and the media that cover them. But we can make some noise. When you see a media outlet running one of these ridiculous stories, call them out on it. Write a letter to the editor, write an op-ed, write something on your frigging MySpace blog, for all I care—just don't let it go unnoticed. When you see a "study" that makes what seems like a dubious claim (women who work get goiters!), check it out. Is the study really saying what the media says it is, or is the media misconstruing the research? Who did the research? (A lot of these studies are funded by conservative organizations with a very clear anti-woman agenda.) And don't forget that these stories exist for a reason—to make women doubt themselves. So don't fall for it.

# 11

# ♀ HE'S A POLITICIAN, SHE'S A FASHION PLATE

**AS IF IT ISN'T HARD ENOUGH BEING A FEMALE POLITICIAN** in a man's world, women in public service have to deal with the extra baggage of being judged constantly on their looks. When was the last time you saw a newspaper article on a male politician's suit? Or a television pundit arguing over whether a male politician was showing too much skin? Sounds ridiculous, but it's what women in politics have to deal with every day of their career.

The White House Project, an organization dedicated to getting women into the higher echelons of political power, released a report in 2000 that studied the newspaper coverage of Elizabeth Dole's presidential campaign compared with that of George W. Bush, John McCain, and Steve Forbes. Dole received less coverage overall, especially on the issues, but when it came to "personal" coverage—talking about her personality, clothing, and looks—she received significantly *more* coverage.[1] Shocking.

In a *USA Today* article, president of the White House Project Marie Wilson noted, "Our research shows that when there's one woman in a campaign, the first thing the press notices about her is what she's wearing, what her hair looks like." [2]

But you don't need a study or research to see the disparity in media coverage.

*The New York Times,* for example, had an entire article in 2007 dedicated to women politicians' fashion sense, "Speaking Chic to Power." [3] Because Lord knows there's nothing more to women in politics than whether or not they wear Prada.

My co-blogger Ann Friedman responded to this piece with the astute observation that not only are women in politics simply judged by what they wear, but their clothing is supposed to mark who they are:

> So Pelosi wears a fashionable nipped-waist jacket and she's marked as a swiftly effective political leader. Condoleezza Rice wears boots; she's marked as a dominatrix. Harriet Miers wears eyeliner; she's marked as begging for Bush's attention. And on and on. Men simply have to choose between a black, navy, or gray suit and pick out a tie. And the color of their cravat rarely marks them as anything. [4]

(Ann also wrote a hilarious post in which she did a critique of male politicians' fashion choices in the same manner that so many do to women: "Can we lose the early-'80s creepy camp counselor glasses, please? It looks like you still live in your mom's basement. And you better be asking for either a chin-tuck or a membership to 24 Hour Fitness this holiday season." [5])

Or just take a look at the way Hillary Clinton has been treated as a presidential candidate—or even as a senator or First Lady. The focus has disproportionately been on her hair, her suits—hell, even her supposed "cleavage"! Seriously. *The Washington Post* in 2007 devoted an entire article to how Clinton was showing tit.

> She was talking on the Senate floor about the burdensome cost of higher education. She was wearing a rose-colored blazer over a black top. The neckline sat low on her chest and had a subtle V-shape. The cleavage registered after only a quick glance. No scrunch-faced scrutiny was necessary. There wasn't an unseemly amount of cleavage showing, but there it was. Undeniable.[6]

Dear lord, you mean . . . women have *breasts?!* Though you have to credit Clinton for having a sense of humor about the way people judge women for their looks. After years of being ridiculed for her hairstyles, Clinton struck back when she created a poster for an appearance at the National Beauty Culturists' League Convention that featured different pictures of her hair throughout the years, with the tagline: "Pay attention to your hair, because everyone else will."

In the most recent presidential election, since Hillary is the only woman running, the media has now taken to talking about the appearance of candidates' wives. (Though, of course, coverage of Bill Clinton's appearance is nowhere to be found. . . . )

And, yes, there are times when men's appearance is talked about in terms of politics, but it's usually related to sexism as well. Take, for example, when papers started reporting that John Edwards spent $400 on his haircut. The coverage—especially conservative coverage—was dedicated to mocking him as feminine because he cared about his hair. That's Sexism 101, friends. And even in the rare circumstance when men's appearance and clothing *are* discussed, they're talked about in terms of how "distinguished" or manly they look. (Think George W. Bush in that cock-strong flight suit!)

## So... what to do?

When you see a biased article, write a letter to the editor! Send it around to your friends with a note about how gross and sexist it is. When you hear friends talk about political candidates and someone makes a comment about a woman's appearance—speak out! Don't let it go unnoticed. And take the bull by the horns: Look into organizations that promote women's leadership and political participation. Encourage your friends to run for office. And wear whatever you damn well please.

# 12

# HE'S A ROMEO,
## SHE'S A STALKER

**A GUY THROWS ROCKS AT A GIRL'S WINDOW** in the middle of the night. He won't take no for an answer—he *must* date her! He serenades her, shows up at her classes, waits at her car. These could be scenes from a burgeoning romance or a stalker gone mad—American culture doesn't differentiate, really.

If a woman does those things, however, she's *always* a stalker. A crazy ex-girlfriend. A psycho. Shit, women are called stalkers for even daring to call a guy a couple of times! Never mind that the majority of stalking is done by men, and the majority of victims are women. When it comes to romance, women are the stalkers and men are just ... romantic.

According to the Department of Justice, one out of every twelve women (and one out of every forty-five men) will be stalked in her lifetime. And whether it's men or women who are the victims of stalking, it's overwhelmingly men who are actually *doing* the stalking—almost 90 percent.

Given the statistics, it's pretty ridiculous that there is still a double standard here: When a man stalks, it's often portrayed as just a joke or romance, but almost anything a woman does will be labeled as stalking (or pathetic).

You need not look much further than Hollywood for the stereotypical crazy female. Think of women stalkers in movies: Glenn Close in *Fatal Attraction*, of course, is the most famous. But there's also Demi Moore in *Disclosure*, Rebecca De Mornay in *The Hand That Rocks the Cradle*, Jennifer Jason Leigh in *Single White Female*, or Kathy Bates in *Misery*.

What most of these characters have in common—besides the crazy—is that they're sex-crazed, single gals who just can't wait to get their hands on someone else's man. Even funnier—women stalker characters are often presented in direct opposition to traditional femininity. For example, Glenn Close in *Fatal Attraction* is the crazy-haired businesswoman, while Michael Douglas's wife is the charming stay-at-home mom. Same thing in *Disclosure*. In *Single White Female*, one of the first signs that something is amiss with Jennifer Jason Leigh's character is when a shocked (shocked!) Bridget Fonda catches her masturbating. (You know, 'cause only psychos do that.) It's so predictable, really. Women can be good little girls or crazies.

This kind of strong-women-are-stalkers attitude is also pretty standard in hetero dating rituals. If you call more than a couple of times, you're stalking a guy. If he calls, he's just persistent.

At the end of the day, we're so invested in a romantic ideal that sees men as the pursuers in a relationship that anything that deviates from that is seen as nutso. And, naturally, anything that holds up that man-chasing-woman model is seen as great. Even when it's criminal.

In 2007, I wrote a post on my blog, Feministing.com, about a creepy shirt Wal-Mart was selling that said, "Some call it stalking, I call it love."

The lettering was scrawled across the shirt in what looked like dripping blood. Classy, eh? The shirt, which was available in the men's section, caught the eye of a stalking victim in North Carolina who complained to the store. She wondered what kind of shirt would be next: "'Some say it's rape, I call it hot sex'? Or: 'Some call it domestic violence, I say I'm just teaching her a lesson'?"

In the comments section, I was surprised to find how many people (mostly men) thought the shirt was simply funny. That there was no larger issue there. Let me tell you something—it's not funny. Ever. I was stalked once, and it was one of the scariest things I've ever experienced. The thought of this guy still freaks me out so much, frankly, that (despite my being a big fan of writing anything and everything about my life) I would never get into the details of the situation, because I'm terrified that he might read the book and take that as a sign that I'm interested.

# *So... what to do?*

Take stalking seriously, for one. It's not a joke, and it's not romantic. And, to be candid, it's not really women who are doing it. But I think the bigger issue is trying to dismantle the idea that romance relies on women being chased or women resisting a persistent guy and eventually giving in. That's called rape culture, folks. What's so bad about a romantic ideal where both parties involved are equally excited about the prospect of dating each other? Sounds pretty reasonable to me.

# 13

# HE'S TOUGH, SHE'S A TOMBOY

**I WAS A TOMBOY, NO DOUBT ABOUT IT.** In elementary school I played sports and ran around the playground with the boys, shunning my female peers, who at the time seemed more concerned with Lee press-on nails than with anything else. In junior high, I wore baggy men's jeans and shirts. So sue me—it was fashionable then! It wasn't until high school that I started dressing "feminine" or hanging out with other girls. Lucky for me, no one ever mocked me for being a tomboy. (I was mocked for entirely different reasons, but that's a story for another day.) The little boys in my class, however, who dared to *like* those conversations about Lee press-on nails or who shied away from sports—they had problems. They were called fags, pussies, and sissies. They were called . . . girls.

You see, it was understandable for me to want to be a tomboy and do "boy" things—because men are better, after all. But for a guy to want to be feminine? Unthinkable. Now, while this double standard affects men negatively, it's mired in misogyny—the idea, of course, is that there's nothing worse than being a girl.

Think about it. Girls can wear pants; boys can't wear skirts. Girls can play with trucks, but the minute I caught one of my little boy cousins playing with a doll, he threw it across the room with a look of shame on his face. It's demeaning to be female, and boys learn that from an early age.

Stephen Ducat, who wrote *The Wimp Factor*, says that "femiphobia"—fear of being feminine—affects men's identity acutely from the time that they're children. Ducat writes that "anxious masculinity" makes men so concerned with appearing manly (or unwomanlike) that they'll do just about anything to seem masculine (which is basically anything that isn't feminine).

In fact, society is so unabashed in its hatred of all things feminine that one of the easiest ways to punish men is simply to feminize them. A South Carolina prison has taken to punishing sexually active prisoners by dressing them in pink jumpsuits. An Arizona prison makes its inmates wear pink underwear—all the time. Thai police officers who step out of line? They're forced to wear pink Hello Kitty armbands. Guy friends have even told me of hazing rituals (whether for frats or sports teams) where young men are put in dresses as a way to demean them. My personal favorite? An Australian joke website (because being womanlike is just hilarious) called "Man Cans" features men who act girlie—like by crying at a movie—suddenly growing breasts as punishment. You can't get much clearer than that.

But the consequences of being "a girl" go way past man-boobs and pink underwear. People are actually killed for transgressing gender norms. You need look no further than the violence committed against transgender people every day. And though society looks down on both men and women who identify outside of their assigned gender, there is a special disdain reserved for men who are feminine.

Trans women (folks who are born male but identify as women) are mocked in the media.

Julia Serano, kickass author of *Whipping Girl: A Transsexual Woman on Sexism and the Scapegoating of Femininity*, says that sexism not only targets women for being women, but targets people because of their femininity.

> The idea that masculinity is strong, tough, and natural while femininity is weak, vulnerable, and artificial continues to proliferate, even among people who believe that women and men are equals. People who are feminine, whether they be female, male, and/or transgender, are almost universally demeaned with respect to their masculine counterparts. This scapegoating of those who express femininity can be seen not only in the male-centered mainstream, but also in the queer community, where "effeminate" gay men have been accused of "holding back" the gay rights movement, and where femme dykes have been accused of being the "Uncle Toms" of the lesbian movement.

So it's not just the usual suspects on this one. It seems that we've all bought into hating all things fem.

# So... what to do?

When you're talking about battling straight-up unadulterated misogyny, there's just no easy answer. I mean, how do you stop something that's been generations in the making? I think we have to start with valuing femininity and, by proxy, women. We may not be able to change the world, but we can change our own worlds. Call people out on using words like "sissy" and "pussy." Throw a fit when someone utters the dreaded words, "Don't be (throw like, cry like) a girl." My very feminist dad had his own gaffe: Whenever I did something "girlie," like be afraid of a spider or something, he would say, "Don't be a Mary." Not no more, folks. We have to start with our own lives and the people in them before we can take on the world.

And despite my tomboyish tendencies—which will probably never leave me entirely—I know that it's not being boylike that makes people valuable. It's being yourself—whether that means baseball or manicures, for boys *or* girls.

# 14

# ⚲ HE'S ANGRY,
## ⚲ SHE'S PMSING

**WHILE IN A FIGHT WITH A MAN** (or anyone, for that matter), how many times have you been accused of being "on the rag"? Or being "unreasonable" or "emotional"? I'm guessing plenty. When men are angry, they're just angry. When women are angry, they're on the rag. Or neurotic. Or crazy. Or being PMS-y.

I had a boyfriend not so long ago who, whenever we got into an argument, would accuse me of "going soap opera." "Here comes Telemundo!" he would shout. His (clearly gendered and vaguely racist) insult was supposed to make me feel like my anger wasn't valid—that it was frivolous and silly, that I was being overly dramatic. This was his not-so-subtle way of trying to shut me up—by accusing me of being emotional. (Unlike men, whose anger is always logical, of course.) Unfortunately, calling me out like this often worked. It felt immobilizing to be called dramatic. Even if you *know* you're being reasonable, we've internalized sexism so much, sometimes we even begin to doubt ourselves. Thankfully, that relationship didn't last. But the lesson I learned did.

When men get angry, they're taken seriously. It's assumed that they have a reason to be so upset. But it seems that whenever women have the gall to express anything other than effusive chipperness, we're accused of having PMS or being nuts. Or we're laughed at or mocked ("Calm down, little lady!").

Women, it seems, aren't allowed to be just plain pissed off.

I think that a lot of this comes from the idea that women are supposed to be "feminine" and docile—anger doesn't fit into the sexist ideal of women as quiet and forever smiling. (*Stepford Wives,* anyone?) That's why you'll often hear feminists being accused of being angry right along with being called "manly." It's a way to try to stifle women's anger and, by proxy, our voices.

When you think about it, it makes sense that society—especially men—would want to keep women's anger under wraps. Because—let's face it—we have a lot of stuff to be upset about! Living in a sexist world is no walk in the fucking park. But what better way to ignore sexism than to make women quiet down? If a woman is too nervous about being called neurotic to get angry about things in her own life, how can she speak out against injustices in the world at large? I can't tell you how many times someone has asked me—when they hear that I'm a feminist—*why* I'm so angry. Or told me to lighten up.

If we complain, we're being rude or loud or obnoxious. If we're angry, there must be something wrong with us.

I believe that's why *so* many women direct that anger inward. Instead of getting angry at the beauty industry that tells us we're fat, we diet and develop eating disorders. Instead of fighting with the girl in junior high who pissed us off, we called her a slut behind her back. All because nice girls don't get mad.

And I think we all know that keeping things inside isn't exactly the healthiest way to deal. In fact, a study on women and anger showed that women disproportionately "keep things bottled up" and suffer physically because of it: We get headaches, depression, heart disease, you name it. I'm not saying that anger doesn't affect men's health as well, but men are "allowed" to vent in a healthy way without being mocked or ridiculed. Women aren't. (Think about how many times someone has said it's "cute" when you get angry. For real.)

When women *are* shown as mad or angry, we become caricatures. The pissed-off, man-hating feminist. The neurotic girlfriend. And, of course, nothing says stereotype like the classic racist/sexist combo of the Angry Black Woman. Black women are *constantly* portrayed in the media and elsewhere as perpetually pissy, usually for comedic effect. 'Cause women's anger is funny.

# So... what to do?

Be as pissed off as you want to be. Don't hold back because you think it's unladylike or some such nonsense. We shouldn't be shamed out of our anger. We should be using it. Using it to make change in our own lives, and using it to make change in the lives around us. (I know, I'm cheesy.) So the next time someone calls you emotional, or asks if you're PMSing, call them on their bullshit.

# 15

# HE'S DISTINGUISHED,
## SHE'S DRIVING MISS DAISY

**UNLIKE MEN—WHO ARE CALLED THINGS** like "distinguished" and "gentlemanly" when they get older—women who age are pretty much done for. We're deemed unfuckable and unlovable and, subsequently, useless. (I know—I'm such an optimist.)

It was just last year, when I was twenty-seven, that I found my first gray hair. It was all short and kinky and stood straight up, right above my bangs. I was not amused. Especially since it wasn't actually *me* who found it, but a twenty-two-year-old guy I was flirting with outside of a bar in my neighborhood. He leaned in (and of course I thought he was going in for a kiss) and actually plucked the hair out of my head, exclaiming, "Look, a gray hair—funny!" I decided never to call him. Of course, it wasn't so much the embarrassment factor as it was the recognition that anyone who would feel comfortable plucking things off my head was probably not for me. But I digress.

Moral of the story: As feminist as I am, there was something about that gray hair that completely freaked me out. But in a world where women are judged almost entirely on their looks, and where "hotness" is akin to youth, I guess that's not all that surprising.

I mean, seriously—how many face-lifts, wrinkle creams, youth serums, vaginal tightening surgeries (don't want an old pussy, obviously), and Botox do we need shoved in our faces in order to get the hint? We get it, already: Old or old-looking is bad for women. Youth is good.

Men, on the other hand, can get as old as they want. (It seems that just by virtue of having a penis, they're considered hot.) When men are older and single they're bachelors—not spinsters or old maids, like us. When men go gray, they look serious and distinguished. When women do, people wonder why the hell we haven't dyed our hair. When men's sexuality wanes—or gets a little ... well, limp—they have paid-for-by-insurance Viagra. Which they're using with their younger "trophy wives," of course, because women over childbearing age don't have sex. (But of course those "older" women who *do* put out a sexual vibe are quickly relegated to joke status: They're cougars or MILFs, not actual women with healthy sexuality.)

I think Goldie Hawn's quote in the 1996 movie *The First Wives Club* says it best: "There are only three ages for women in Hollywood—babe, district attorney, and Driving Miss Daisy." The same could be said of women in general—we're young hot things, moms, or old ladies. That's all we got.

And seriously, in what world is it right that Hugh Hefner has, like, seven young "girlfriends" but women like Helen Mirren are considered over the hill?

Honestly, I think a lot of this nonsense is related to the idea that women's main purpose in life should be having children. So if we're too old to have any kids, we don't have a purpose. Just look at the recent media frenzies about those poor old career women who waited too long to have babies. I mean, there are countless books, articles, and television segments on how women who didn't have children soon enough will never have them ever! For example, Sylvia Ann Hewlett's *Creating a Life: Professional Women and the Quest for Children,* which argues that if women in their twenties don't hop to it and find a man and get knocked up, they'll end up old and barren, got a ridiculous amount of media play. Never mind that Hewlett never talks about the fact that (gasp!) some women don't want children, and that study after study shows that waiting to have kids means better health for moms and babies. Better that we scare the bejesus out of women.

Not to mention how men get off easy—no one ever mentions that older men have an increased chance of having children with genetic disorders. And no one scoffs when men refuse to date (seriously, I've seen this in many a singles ad) women over thirty-five because they're "less fertile."

But, of course, double standards about age don't end with looks, sex, and babies. If only. The average income for men over sixty-five in the United States is about $14,000 more than the average income for women over sixty-five. And older women are the poorest of the poor in this country—mostly because of not having social security after long lives of taking care of husbands, or because women are more likely to hold low-income positions that offer no pension benefits.

## So... what to do?

How can we battle a double standard that is so pervasive? I say defy it. Or embrace it. I would love to see folks reclaiming the word "spinster"; I always thought it had a certain something. One of my favorite poems about age is "Warning," by Jenny Joseph, who says: "When I am an old woman I shall wear purple / With a red hat which doesn't go, and doesn't suit me." (The poem also talks about learning to spit—that's what sold me.) So I say, screw them. Older women are hot; women do not become useless once we can't (or don't want to) have children. So let's start by not judging ourselves anymore. Wrinkle cream begone, and fuck Botox. Though I have to admit, if many more of these grays pop up, you'll be seeing me at the hair salon. But don't worry—I'll wear purple.

*If you want to know more about how to fight ageism and sexism, check out the Older Women's League (OWL).*

# 16

# ⚡ HE'S MANLY,
## SHE'S SASQUATCH

**WHEN I WAS ABOUT TWENTY-THREE,** I took a vacation to Spain (it was awesome). While on a ferry from Barcelona to Ibiza, I started chatting with a young Australian guy. When I mentioned being a feminist, he lifted my arm and looked underneath—as if to check for underarm hair. (He didn't find any.) I was not amused. The whole feminists-are-hairy stereotype is just so old school and ridiculous. But what also irritated me was the idea that if I happened to *not* be shaved, it was some sort of huge beauty and fashion faux pas.

There is a clear double standard when it comes to men, women, and hair removal. Now, perhaps you think shaving and waxing is a vapid issue to bring up, considering the more serious double standards of pay inequity, sexuality, and the like. But the fact is, spending the better part of your life having to shave huge areas of your body just to be considered not disgusting *is* a big deal.

The first-ever advertisement for a hair-removal product for women was featured in a 1915 *Harper's Bazaar,* and depicted a woman in a sleeveless gown with perfectly smooth pits. Razor sales soon skyrocketed. (Waxing became popular with the advent of the bikini, Brazilian waxing—who knows?)

I don't think I started shaving until I was in junior high, but I wanted to earlier. I'm Italian, after all, and dark, coarse hair is in my genes. There was something so humiliating about wearing shorts to school and seeing all of my hairless-legged peers. I remember in fifth grade stealing my mom's razor and taking off a small strip on my calf—just to see what would happen. (I was thrilled to see that despite my mom's tales of hair growing back thicker and darker, all was well on my stubbly strip.) But now, thinking about those days when my underarms were raw, my legs filled with nicks, or my delicates chapped from my first bikini wax (dear god, ouch), I'm just pissed. Pissed that I felt the overwhelming need to conform, pissed that guys don't have to go through the same thing, pissed that to this day I still don't feel right if my underarms aren't shaved. (If it's winter and I'm not showing off the legs, they're au naturel—sorry, just don't care that much.)

Sure, there is a somewhat new trend of men getting shaved and waxed. (Who could forget the chest-waxing scene in *The 40-Year-Old Virgin?*) The difference is, however, that men getting trimmed—or manscaped, as I've heard it called—is considered an extra hygienic step. It's not necessary. If men don't get waxed, plucked, and shaved, no one is going to think they're "dirty" or not taking care of themselves. Not so much with women. Anyone who recalls the brouhaha that ensued after Julia Roberts showed up to a 1999 film premiere sporting a sleeveless red dress and underarm fuzz knows what I'm taking about. There was mockery, jokes, and disbelief. If women don't remove their hair, they're to be laughed at. Or pitied.

This isn't to say that I'm against hair removal altogether—after all, I still do it, so who am I to judge? But I am pretty disturbed by the idea that if women don't shave, we're dirty or gross. And that the hair-removal trend is hitting younger and younger women.

For example, take Nair, the depilatory-cream creator. In 2007 Nair introduced a new product line: Nair Pretty, aimed at ten- to fifteen-year-olds—what the industry calls "first-time hair removers." (Does that "first-time" line give anyone else the heebie-jeebies?) The Nair Pretty marketing scheme is half hilarious, half terrifying. Hilarious because of the obvious attempt to speak to young people in contrived slang: "It's not that you're obsessed or anything, but maybe you've noticed that the hair on your legs (and other parts of your body) is just a little bit thicker and darker than before. Chill. You're growing up . . . it's all good." I almost expected the next line to be about "getting jiggy" with hair removal. But it's still terrifying, because the message of Nair Pretty is that you can't be pretty unless you're taking care of that unsightly leg (and everywhere else) hair. And, as gossip blog Gawker put it when they covered the product line, "we're probably months away from Baby Brazilians."

In fact, bloggers aren't the only ones worried about young women removing their hair (which is presumably related to sex, though I did it when I was younger just so I wouldn't be mocked). A Missouri State Senate bill in 2006 proposed parental consent for girls under the age of eighteen wanting Brazilian bikini waxes. Kind of over the top, I admit, but there is something creepy about the idea of girls who are barely old enough to have sex going out and messing with their na-nas.

# So... what to do?

Rethink the hair-as-dirty paradigm. It exists solely to make us feel shitty about ourselves and to make money from the beauty industry. Even if you shave and wax every hair except the ones on your head, think about *why* it's so important to you to be hairless. Or, if you're up for it, take a cue from stand-up comedian Shazia Mirza, who made a New Year's resolution not to shave anymore: "I have decided that enough is enough and I have decided to just grow it, grow it like grass and try and live with it.... Every woman has hair. This is a fact.... It's about time hair on women was celebrated, not condemned.... A woman can definitely be sexy in a pair of Jimmy Choos and a pair of hairy legs, she can be sexy in a Wonderbra and hairy armpits, and she can be very hot in a miniskirt and hairy arms." [1]

# 17

# HE'S SUCCESSFUL,
## SHE'S A SHOWOFF

**I MAKE MORE MONEY THAN MY BOYFRIEND.** A good deal more. (It doesn't hurt that I have five years on him.) This means that I tend to pick up the check more often than he does—especially because I'm a big, *big* fan of eating out. He, on the other hand, is happy to eat boxed mac and cheese five nights a week. This doesn't cause problems in our relationship—it actually works out for the both of us. But according to dating "experts" and societal expectations, I'm breaking the rules. I'm "emasculating" my boyfriend by not letting him take care of me. Or something.

Though of course, if I were dating someone whom I consistently let treat me and pay my way on dates, I'd be a gold digger, or a "dinner whore." There's just no winning when it comes to cash and romance. (If you're a woman, of course.)

A September 2007 article in *The New York Times* explored the supposedly recent trend of successful young women making more money than their significant others and how it has affected their dating lives: "Women are encountering forms of hostility they weren't prepared to meet, and are trying to figure out how to balance pride in their accomplishments against their perceived need to bolster the egos of the men they date."

Bolstering egos ... seriously? Is masculinity so damn fragile that it can't handle being treated to dinner? I can understand some men who have bought into the whole I-need-to-take-care-of-my-woman crap feeling a tab uncomfortable with being treated, but "hostility"?

It's kind of amazing how tied up men's sense of self is with their ability to "care for" women. When I discussed this article on Feministing.com, one male commenter (who shall remain nameless) wrote, "How could a guy ever feel needed in a relationship where his partner completely outperformed him?" Wowza. Hear that, ladies? Don't let on that you're *too* successful, or your man may run scared!

Sounds silly, but that's almost exactly what this *New York Times* article was saying: "For men, it is accepted, even desirable, to flaunt their high status. Not so for many women." (Another double standard, I guess. Men are proud of their accomplishments; women are braggarts!)

But it's not just trend pieces in the Style section that are addressing dating etiquette. Take this charming segment from CBS, for example: "Reviving Dating Rules." Along the same don't-emasculate-through-success-and-confidence lines, dating "expert" April Beyer says that women should never pay for dates while in the courting process and never ask men out. Because it would interfere with their hunter instincts or some such shit.

I'm hoping that women haven't really bought into this tripe. I mean, do we *really* still believe that women need to be taken care of? Or are we so ashamed of our accomplishments that we're willing to "dumb down" our smarts and successes so as to not hurt the delicate male ego?

Then, of course, there's the other side of the "who pays?" debate. Women who happily and readily accept dinners and gifts, who follow the "rules," are often called out as gold diggers. The term "dinner whore" is a newer one—unlike the gold digger, who marries for cash, the dinner whore goes on dates simply for the free meals and entertainment.

On Urban Dictionary, a "dinner whore" is defined as follows: "a girl who is exclusively after a free meal or an expensive gift. She actively seeks out dates with well-off men who will wine and dine her at upscale restaurants." The idea that women are somehow taking advantage of men via dates even got itself an article in the *New York Post*. The oh-so-classy title: "Meet the Dinner Whores."

Charming. Is there seriously a new trend of women going out with men simply for the luxury of a free meal? I doubt it. But it's a great way of painting women who dare to follow the traditional dating rules as whores. We can't win either way.

Dinner whore or emasculating billpayer, I think what depresses me most about this double standard actually is the idea that money is so tied up with our notions of romance and dating. It's a stark reminder that women are still commodified and that when we try to exercise any kind of power in a relationship, we're punished.

# So... *what to do?*

I think the answer to this one is actually quite simple: Let each relationship or date speak for itself. There doesn't have to be a hard and fast rule when it comes to romance—just do what feels right. If someone makes more money and wants to go to a nicer restaurant, let that person pay and leave power relations at the door. That's not about gender, it's math. But there is one rule to follow, gals. Don't date anyone who feels slighted by the idea of you treating. Frankly, anyone who isn't comfortable with women being up-front about their financial success probably won't be comfortable with other successes as well. There's a sexism there that's impossible to ignore.

# 18

# ☂ HE'S SUPERDAD,
## SHE'S SHITTYMOM

**MOMS CAN NEVER REALLY DO ENOUGH.** They can never be too selfless, too devoted, or too giving. They can never go to enough soccer games or school plays. They can never be perfect—though that's what society demands of them. Women are expected to be stellar moms, but if dads so much as go to a baseball game or read their kid a bedtime story, they're frigging father of the year. It's the parenting double standard, and it looks like it's here to stay.

My mother did (and still does, to some degree) everything for my sister and me. She cooked, cleaned, took care of us when we were sick, played with us, disciplined us—the whole shebang. My dad was there, too; he was an amazing father. He was our Brownie leader, our reader of nighttime stories and singer of songs. But the kudos he got for doing half as much as my mother did were pretty incredible. For my mom to spend all of her time caring for us—well, that was just expected.

Now, traditional norms about who should be the caregiver of children (ahem, women) are nothing new. But what is more recent is the idea that caregiver women must be *perfect* moms, and the setting up of impossible-to-meet standards for mothers. Susan J. Douglas and

Meredith W. Michaels, authors of *The Mommy Myth: The Idealization of Motherhood and How It Has Undermined Women,* call this the "new momism":

> ... the insistence that no woman is truly complete or fulfilled unless she has kids, that women remain the best primary care-takers of children, and that to be a remotely decent mother, a woman has to devote her entire physical, psychological, emotional, and intellectual being, 24/7, to her children.

And, of course, the impossible standards serve a purpose—they mean that the media, the public, or even your own family can beat up on women constantly for not living up to this new momism.

If we work outside the home, we're neglecting our kids and turning them into bullies. If we're white, that is. If we're not white, we're "welfare queens" who should be working. Working women think we can "have it all." Fathers who work, on the other hand, are being responsible providers. If we stay at home, we're lazy. We're supposed to breastfeed—but not for too long and for God's sake not in public. We have to be straight. Most of all, we have to be married.

If we're (gasp!) single, and have a child deliberately without a man, well, we're just selfish and preparing that kid for a lifetime of misery. When Louise Sloan, author of *Knock Yourself Up: A Tell-All Guide to Becoming a Single Mom,* was interviewed on Salon.com—telling the story of her own insemination when she was forty-one years old, and the stories of other women who became single moms by choice—she was slammed with horrible comments: " ... the boy will be screwed up or resent women, not having had a father around. He will have a higher chance of being a criminal. ... He will likely understand that all the feminist piffle shoved in his head is the opposite of what men need to know to be *effective* and happy free agents in the bigger world. . . . Your child will grow up fatherless and disadvantaged. But you got what you want, and that is what is most important. How sad." Charming, huh? All for just wanting a baby.

Then, of course, if you *don't* want to have kids at all, you're also selfish. You know, because all women are supposed to want children. If we don't, then we're either dismissed ("Oh, you'll want kids someday!") or scorned.

Dads, on the other hand . . . well, they have it pretty nice. If they manage to show up and financially support their kid, they're automatically a good dad. (And this isn't to say that limiting fathers' roles to a financial one is a good thing—it's just another way traditional gender roles fuck things up. If a father stays at home to take care of his children or is doting, he's lazy or not a "real" man.) Dads who leave work early to catch a kid's school play or baseball game get props for being *so* involved in their kid's life, while their female counterparts get called slackers.

But it's not just about workplace and domestic issues when it comes to blaming Mom. Now, even the law is stepping in. Just recently, a woman in Connecticut was convicted of risk of injury to a minor because her son committed suicide and the courts said she should have seen it coming. And "fetal protection" laws are making it easier to arrest women for having stillborn babies—it happened in Utah to a woman who refused to have a cesarean section.

# So... what to do?

Making women to blame for all things baby isn't exactly new—so it's no easy battle to fight. But there are things we can do. For one, don't fall into the trap of identifying yourself by whether or not you have children—and don't let others do it either! Find out about your workplace rights: No one has the right to discriminate against you if you have children. Fight for childcare! The "care crisis" is a real thing—and it's not just a personal problem, it's a political one. The United States is the only industrialized nation that doesn't have paid maternity leave; this has to change. Don't expect to be perfect. No one is a perfect mother (except you, Mom!), and the standards that tell you as much exist because of sexism. So screw them.

# 19

# HE'S THE BOSS,
## SHE'S A BITCH

**IF YOU'RE A WOMAN IN A POSITION OF POWER,** you've probably been called a bitch. (Well, chances are if you're any woman *at all* you've been called a bitch, but I digress.) Or maybe you've been called a "boss lady." Or a ball buster, ball breaker, or some other word that means castrating, pushy, loud, and basically out of line. Why out of line? Because women don't belong in positions of power, silly! So if you've gotten there, you must be a bitch. Men, though, are natural bosses.

Just think of the way men and women in the workplace are described. Men are ambitious, women are ruthless; men are commanding, women are bossy; men who leave work early to get to a kid's soccer game are devoted dads, women who do the same are slacking off. An ABC News article from 2006 on workplace double standards had this great example: "When Russell Crowe tossed a heavy phone at a hotel clerk, we were mildly amused at his impatience. When Naomi Campbell threw a cell phone at her assistant, she was labeled an out-of-control prima donna. Both stars misbehaved, but our societal bias caused us to be a lot more critical of Campbell. Not fair."[1] Indeed.

It's the boss versus the bitch, and the ladies are losing.

You need look no further than the movie industry to see how "working women" (as if we don't all work in some capacity or another) are thought of. One of my favorite writers (and people), Rebecca Traister, took on the boss-lady caricature in a review of the 2006 movie *The Devil Wears Prada:*

> What else but the male erotic nightmare (Michael Crichton's, to be exact) could have produced Demi Moore's duplicitous (and horny!) Meredith Johnson, who puts the moves on Michael Douglas and then accuses him of sexual harassment in *Disclosure?* Jane Craig, Holly Hunter's immensely likable but totally neurotic producer in *Broadcast News,* forces herself to cry every morning before work. Diane Keaton's *Baby Boom* executive J.C. Watts has a corner office, a six-figure salary, and a loveless relationship; they call her "Tiger Lady"—rowr! Check out Glenn Close as live-action fashion queen Cruella DeVil in *101 Dalmations:* She berates peons, asks an assistant, "What kind of sycophant are you?" (reply: "What kind of sycophant do you want me to be?"), opines that "We lose more women to marriage than war, famine, and disease!"

You know, 'cause being powerful and being feminine (meaning a mother and wife) just aren't compatible. But it's not just Hollywood and harmless workplace banter. The bitch/boss double standard is more pervasive than you'd like to think—and it affects women and work.

A 2007 MSNBC survey showed that women in leadership positions haven't made much progress in their attempts to fight workplace bias. Most respondents—men and women—actually said they would prefer a male boss and think that men are more effective leaders.

Those surveyed used words like "moody," bitchy," "gossipy," and "emotional" to describe women bosses. The most popular term for women in power? "Catty."[2]

Oh, how I *hate* the word "catty." And "catfight." I mean, when men are competitive they're called just that. When women are competitive, we're subject to tired lines like "Kitty's got claws!" It's just another way to diminish and demean the idea of women having power. Really, what better way to dismiss female competition and power than to give it a cutesy animal name?

The other, more nefarious intention is to make power seem unattractive to women. After all, if all women in power are bitches, then why would younger women aspire to be someone with power? Much like the anti-feminist stereotypes (man-hating, ugly, and so on) that exist to keep women away from an awesome political movement that could improve their lives, calling women bosses bitches is strategic. Not only does it put women who are already in power "in their place," but it also serves to deter women who are on the fast track from being too successful, too ambitious, too . . . well, bosslike.

The other deliberate (though sneaky) way to make power seem unattractive is to call women bosses men or menlike. You can't be feminine and in power! (You need not look further than all the faux media trends that say women who work outside of the home have fucked-up kids or unhappy lives, despite the fact that real studies show just the opposite.) You have to wear shoulder pads and scoff at your kids as you drop them off at daycare while yelling at your emasculated husband. What's sneaky about this one is that it not only stereotypes women bosses as butch, but it also defines characteristics of power as inherently male.

# So... what to do?

I have a feeling that it's going to be a long time before men (and other women) will stop calling powerful women bitches. So while we're waiting . . . work! Be successful! And take being called a bitch as a compliment. Because it means you're doing something right.

# 20

# HE'S WELL PAID, SHE'S SCREWED

**THE WAGE GAP MAY BE THE MOST INTERESTING** double standard there is, just in that it's so obviously ridiculously unfair, yet little seems to ever be done about it. Men get paid more than women for doing the same job. Period. There's no sugarcoating that! Yet it's something we tacitly accept every day when we go to work. Now *that* is scary.

Women now earn 77 cents to a male's dollar. Not such a huge improvement over the years, considering we were earning 60 cents to the dollar when the Equal Pay Act was signed in 1963. In fact, sometimes it seems like things are never going to get better wage-wise. A report by the American Association of University Women, for example, found that women who were one year out of college earned 80 percent of what their male counterparts did—but that those same women ten years after graduation were earning just 69 cents to the male dollar. And this was the same for women who attended shmancy schools, for women who chose different kinds of jobs—there was just an "unexplained" wage gap.[1] (Cough, sexism, cough.) Then, of course, you take into account the additional discrimination that comes along with being a woman who isn't white . . . and that gap gets even wider.

It seems unbelievable that in this day and age, employers would just be sexist assholes for no reason whatsoever. ("She has a vagina? Well, knock 10K off her starting salary!") I think it's the ingrained sexism that fucks women at work, especially the assumption that women don't *need* to make as much money—you know, 'cause they probably have a man at home (or Daddy) taking care of them. The other issue, when it comes to giving men promotions and paying them more, is that having a family tends to work in favor of men, while it works *against* women's best interest. Employers may think that men "have a family to support" and therefore need the extra money. But because of gendered stereotypes they would never think the same thing about a woman employee, 'cause, hey, ladies aren't supposed to be the breadwinners, right?

Then there's the "old boys' club." Men make a lot of their work moves on the golf course—there's no limit to men's outside-of-work networking opportunities. And let's face it, women just aren't going to get invited to that baseball game or night out at the strip club. Sara Laschever, coauthor of *Women Don't Ask: The High Cost of Avoiding Negotiation—and Positive Strategies for Change,* says· "Women absolutely need to network with each other and with friendly and approachable men, as well. Women tend to be excluded from or peripheral to many of the social and professional networks in which men exchange information about what to ask for, who to ask, when to ask, how to ask. Women need to find ways into those networks if they're going to gain access to all that information."[2]

Laschever's book deals mostly with the issue of whether or not women speak up enough about what they want out of their jobs. While some argue that women should just be asking for raises more (which is undoubtedly true), because of workplace sexism, being up-front about your salary needs doesn't always pay off. A 2007 study found that women were less likely to ask for raises because the social costs were much greater for them than for their male coworkers. Which basically is a throwback to the original workplace double standard for women: If you're aggressive about anything, you're a bitch. Linda C. Babcock, a professor of economics at Carnegie Mellon University who conducted the study, was quoted in *The Washington Post* as saying that "men were always less willing to work with a woman who had attempted to negotiate than with a woman who did not.... They always preferred to work with a woman who stayed mum. But it made no difference to the men whether a guy had chosen to negotiate or not."[3] Shocking, huh? We're given shit for not asking for more raises, but when we do we're pariahs.

Now, whenever you talk about the wage double standard, the conservatives come out in droves to whine about how it's not *really* sexism that makes for women's lower salaries—it's all the women who choose to work part-time or stay at home and take care of the kiddies. (We *want* to be earning less money, obviously.) To which you must call bullshit. Because all of the research done on the wage gap—usually by the Census Bureau—studies women who work full-time, all year. It doesn't include salary information about women who took time off to have babies. So enough of that excuse. It's time to move forward and stop letting the guys take all the cash.

# So... what to do?

Know your worth! And make sure that you're earning what you should be. There's no shame in asking around your workplace about who is making what. So if you find out that your male coworkers who do the same job as you are making more money, do something about it. If you see men being promoted over women for no discernible reason, speak out. And be proactive! There's a new trend among working women in some cities to start all-women networking events. (*The Wall Street Journal* even reported that events like these are getting support from business clients, who *like* doing work with companies that take diversity seriously.) But I think some of the best advice comes from Laschever, who told Feministing.com interviewer Celina, "I always say, ask for more and ask often."

# **HE'S GAY, SHE'S A FANTASY**

**ASK A STRAIGHT GUY ABOUT LESBIANS,** and you're likely to get some smart-ass comment about porn, girl-on-girl action, or how they don't mind them so long as they can "join in." Charming. Ask about gay men, however, and it seems the only appropriate response is disgust. When it comes to being queer, gay men are gross and lesbians are hot (so long as they look like cheerleaders and fuck men too, of course).

While this double standard is undoubtedly bad for gay men, it's just as (if not more) insulting to gay women. The assumption behind the hypocrisy is that lesbians aren't "really" gay and they don't have "real" sex. The idea being, of course, that if a dick isn't involved, it's just not real sex. I can't tell you how many times I've heard this sentiment repeated by friends who I thought knew better; I'm sure you have, too. Lesbians aren't a threat to their all-precious manhood so long as men can keep pretending that all gay women are like the gals in porn movies. (You know, where butch women just don't exist.)

I'm actually reminded of a *Saturday Night Live* sketch with Joshua Jackson where a bunch of frat boys wish on some magic monkey claw or something (don't ask) to see "real live lesbian sex," and all of a sudden are brought to the bedroom of a butch gay couple breaking out the patchouli oil.

# 21

Faux male-friendly lesbianism is becoming so trendy, folks are even writing songs about it. "My Girl Got a Girlfriend," by Ray-L, is the epitome of dismissiveness when it comes to queer women. The chorus goes: "My girl gotta girlfriend / I just found out but it's aight / Long as I can be wit her too . . . Cuz havin two chicks is better than no chicks / I'd rather just join in / Keep my girl and keep the other one too." You have to love the assumption that *of course* two women would want a man to join in their sex.

So what's the deal? Why the fear of gay men but the acceptance of lesbians? (And let's be honest—society's acceptance standards tend to be formed by what's acceptable to straight white dudes.) A *Time* magazine article about Ellen DeGeneres's success noted, "Lesbians simply don't inspire the kind of social-sexual unease that gay men do. Two chicks kissing is a male fantasy, a sweeps stunt. Two dudes kissing is gross-out humor. It's Sacha Baron Cohen open-mouthing Will Ferrell in *Talladega Nights*. It's a million *Brokeback Mountain* jokes. It's the Snickers Super Bowl ad, in which two mechanics locked lips while sharing a candy bar. (Or, as Freud might have said, a "candy bar.") Even in post–*Queer Eye* pop culture, lesbians can choose lovers; gay men can choose drapes."

(That Snickers commercial was actually the most homophobic thing I've seen on television in a while, by the way. After two men's lips accidentally touch while they are eating a Snickers, they proceed to bash each other's heads in and bang on stuff to prove that they're "still men." Paging Dr. Freud!)

So really, at the end of the day, this double standard is completely tied up with men's fear of being feminized! Whether it's through appropriating lesbianism as a straight man's dream or bashing on gay men, straight guys get to reaffirm how masculine they are. It would be sad if it weren't so horrifying. Because while it may not seem like such a big deal if guys want to get all revved up about faux lesbians and skeeved by gay men, the consequences of this kind of prejudice can be more than just a few jokes. Lesbian women who are raped are often targeted because of their sexuality and told that they just need a "real man." Men who are gay-bashed are similarly targeted—because they pose a threat to straight sexuality.

# So... what to do?

Call people out on their bullshit. This double standard is particularly pervasive because of porn culture and the like. So be on the lookout and don't let it go uncommented on.

# 22

# HE'S HIMSELF,
## SHE'S MRS. HIMSELF

**I USED TO WANT TO TAKE MY MOM'S LAST NAME** in addition to my dad's. It seemed wrong to me that her last name just got lost in the wind, like it never existed. (Though I ended up deciding that Jessica Michelucci-Valenti was just too much of a mouthful to deal with. Go figure.)

The last-name debacle is definitely something I've written about before, because it's one of those double standards that are so *obviously* ridiculous and sexist—yet so accepted—that it bears repeating!

Now, most American women who marry men will change their last name (note I didn't say "maiden name"; if that were the case, we'd all lose our second names upon doing the nasty) to their husband's. That's just a fact. So I have no illusions about creating some sort of mass revolt of women keeping their own last names (though that would be nice!), but I do think an examination of the last-name double standard is warranted—especially when it seems that the powers that be have such a stake in making sure that things stay the same.

The reason I hear most often when women talk about why they want to take their spouse's last name is tradition. To which I say, *meh.* I'm unimpressed. There are plenty of traditions worth keeping. Saturday brunch with the girls. For you fellow Italians, making Sunday gravy.

Birthday cake. (It's no coincidence that my notions of traditions are all about food. I like me some good meals, what can I say?) But holding on to traditions that not only make your life more difficult—legally changing your last name, and all the paperwork that goes along with it—but are also mired in sexist ideals of women being owned? That's just too much. (Quick remedial lesson on last names for those not in the know: The idea is that women were passed as property from father to husband; we don't really have an identity of our own—just that which the men in our lives define for us.) The other reasons women give for changing their last names run the gamut from "it's better for the kids" to "hyphenation is too difficult," and so on. Yet, as friend and fellow feminist blogger Amanda Marcotte points out, you rarely see men using these excuses to change their last names to their wives'!

> [I]f you think a name change is necessary, you can have the man change his name. It's an elegant solution. Not only do you have all the perceived benefits, but you are sticking it to the patriarchy. This solution even works if you're employing the "I don't like my last name anyway" thing, because if there's a lot of people out there who dislike their last names, then the odds are strongly in favor of the fact that half of them will be men. But for some reason, when this discussion comes up, women and women only seem to dislike their last names.

Interestingly enough, when men *do* try to change their last names to their wives', they run into all kinds of obstacles. (And apparently men *are* doing this more and more, at least says *USA Today.* Nice!)[1] If a man wants to change his name after he gets married, only seven states in the United States allow him to do so without going through a ridiculous, expensive, and long legal process that women in the same position *don't* have to go through.

Take Michael Buday, for example, in California. Buday went to the Department of Motor Vehicles to change his last name to his wife's, and not only was he ridiculed by the staff there(!), he also found out that the hoops he would have to jump through were out of control: a $300 court fee, six times as much as the fee for women, and he would have to advertise his name change in a newspaper. WTF? Luckily, the ACLU of Southern California took up his case and is seeking to change the law in the state. But it makes you think: If changing your last name to your hubby's is "no big deal," then why is the government so hell-bent on making sure the opposite doesn't happen? It has a vested interest in keeping women in traditional gender roles—and the last-name thing is a huge part of that, and a part of maintaining patriarchal family structures.

# So... what to do?

I've said it before, and I'll say it again—keep your last name! Or choose a new one. Or hyphenate. I just don't see any reason to do otherwise. That's not to say I think you're a bad feminist if you do choose to take a man's last name. But if you do, be honest about it. Don't say it's because it's tradition or because you don't like your last name. As Amanda noted, just be honest that it's sexist: "So are high heels and I wear those. Hell, I wear those despite the complaints of boyfriends in the past who preferred displays of female subservience that didn't slow down how fast we could walk. We're all guilty, so that's not the issue. The issue is the amount of effort put into pretending that the name change isn't sexist." Word.

# 23

# HE'S GETTING AN EDUCATION,
## SHE'S GETTING IN HIS WAY

**WOMEN ARE DOING AMAZING THINGS EDUCATION-WISE.** We're going to and graduating from college in higher numbers than ever—same with getting master's degrees. We're even bigger in numbers than men in higher education. Given that we're kicking so much ass in school, can someone tell me why women are still underrepresented in high-level and managerial positions once we enter the workforce?

According to the Department of Education, about three in every ten boys who go to college get out four years later with a degree; four out of ten girls do.[1] And as of 2005, a little over 57 percent of bachelor's degrees were earned by women, a little over 42 percent by men. (The numbers were pretty much flipped back in 1970.)[2] Not too shabby, eh?

But apparently, women's doing so well in school has some people freaked out—the worry is that if women do well, men do poorly. In fact, the mere fact that women are doing better in terms of education has prompted the media and conservative organizations to declare a full-on "boy crisis"!

Article after article for the last five years or so has bemoaned the decrease in men getting bachelor's degrees—and most of the blame has been put on feminists. It seems that because of women's rights, boys are being discouraged from doing well in school—at all levels. How could something like women fighting for equality mess boys up in grade school? Well, it seems we've feminized learning. Or something.

Take, for example, seventeen-year-old Doug Anglin of Massachusetts, who filed a federal discrimination suit claiming that his high school discriminates against boys. Anglin complains that "the system is designed to the disadvantage of males.... From the elementary level, they establish a philosophy that if you sit down, follow orders, and listen to what they say, you'll do well and get good grades. Men naturally rebel against this." Which explains why guys flee from hierarchical structures like the army. Uh, wait.... Anglin also complained that when teachers are grading homework, they give extra points to students who decorate their notebooks—a policy that *clearly favors* girls, because everyone knows that gluesticks are for pussies. My favorite article about this lawsuit, in *The Boston Globe,* has the most telling quote of them all: "Larry O'Connor, another Milton High senior who supports Anglin ... said he is surrounded by a sea of girls in his classes."[3] Noooo! They're everywhere! It seems that, like this lawsuit, a lot of complaints about the "boy crisis" have more to do with women doing well and being strong in numbers than with men *not* doing well. As Katha Pollitt said in a 2006 column, maybe these boys "will just have to learn to learn in a room full of smart females."[4] You know, suck it up.

Anti-feminist whining aside, what's truly interesting is that there really is no boy crisis. It's been debunked as a media myth over and over again. A 2006 *Washington Post* article noted, "Although low-income boys, like low-income girls, are lagging behind middle-class students, boys are scoring significant gains in elementary and middle school and are much better prepared for college. . . . Much of the pessimism about young males seems to derive from inadequate research, sloppy analysis, and discomfort with the fact that although the average boy is doing better, the average girl has gotten ahead of him."[5] The real education crisis is that people of color and low-income children are worse off. White dudes are still going as strong as they ever were, thank you very much.

But while the media and anti-feminists continue about a faux boy crisis, they're silent on the continued disparity in jobs at the top and in advanced and professional degrees. (Because that would interrupt their boys-as-victims-of-feminism diatribe.)

Women still earn significantly fewer advanced degrees in business, engineering, and computer science than men (and these are the degrees that lead to much higher-paying jobs); men outnumber women in earning doctorates and professional degrees. And while nearly half of all law students are women there are nowhere near as many female law partners, professors, and judges as there are men in these positions. The same bodes true for women in managerial positions, high-level decision-making positions, and CEO spots.[6]

It seems that sexism and discrimination follow us through the workforce, no matter how well we're faring in school.

# So... what to do?

Think about going to school for engineering, for starters! Too often, women are pushed into programs that don't necessarily lead to high-paying jobs. This isn't to say that you shouldn't follow your bliss and all that, but try to follow the cash too! If you're a college student, find out what your university's gender breakdown is in terms of tenured professors, or how many women are involved in traditionally male fields. And put that information out there! When you hear someone talk about the supposed boy crisis, set them straight. Let them know that just because girls are doing well, it doesn't mean that boys are doing worse. Encourage your girlfriends to go for advanced degrees and not stop at a BA. And when you're in the workforce and you see that glass ceiling you're about to hit, make some noise about it.

# 24

# ♀ HE'S INDEPENDENT,
## SHE'S PATHETIC

**WHEN WAS THE LAST TIME YOU WENT TO A MOVIE BY YOURSELF?** Or out to eat? Or to another country? If it was recently, kudos. I hate the idea that women shouldn't do things on their own (for safety reasons) or that if we do (like go to a bar alone) we're pathetic. But for some reason, the notion that ladies shouldn't leave the house unless they're escorted by a man is still going strong.

If a man is out to dinner alone, it's normal. If a woman is, she must be waiting for someone, or she's been stood up, or she's lonely. Ditto for going to the movies alone. And if a woman travels alone? She's putting herself in danger! It's like we're living in this bizarre universe where the very simple act of walking around (or sitting around) by ourselves *means* something. It means we're targets, or pathetic, or anything other than just, well, being alone like a normal person.

Have you ever been sitting by yourself—reading in a park, drinking at the bar, whatever—and a guy comes up to you? What the fuck is that? It's like just by virtue of not having male company with you, you're open for business? I've even been in a bar with girlfriends—like, a big group of girlfriends—just to have some asshole come up and ask why we're alone. Huh? So because we're not in the presence of cock, we're "alone"? (I know you ladies know what I'm talking about.)

I mean, even just living alone for the first time was an interesting experience for me. After getting my first apartment without roommates, I had relatives ask me if I was going to get a dog for protection (I did, but Monty is not tough enough to protect anyone) or when, oh when, I was going to get married already. My guy friends have been living alone for years. But I guess they're "independent." Me, I'm halfway down spinster road.

While doing research on this particular double standard, I came across an amazing/terrifying article from *The New York Times* circa 1908. The headline was "Women's Right to Eat Alone." Because, apparently, it wasn't always legal!

> The Women's Republican Club, at its regular meeting at the Plaza yesterday afternoon, put itself as on record as opposing the opening of saloons on Sundays and also as believing that women should be permitted to eat in public places when and where they please.

While trying to garner support for this bill that would allow women to eat in restaurants without a male escort, one of the club members was quoted as saying, "I believe it is a protection to all decent women that women alone should not be allowed to eat in public restaurants."

I bring this up because despite its being a quote from 1908, it's not so far off from some of the arguments you'll hear even today against women doing things by their lonesome.

For example, how there's still a ton of victim blaming going on when it comes to rape victims. Women who were walking home *alone*, who were at the bar *alone,* or the like, are often questioned about why they would walk around by themselves—as if we shouldn't be free to walk around alone without fear of assault! (But it's about protecting women, they swear.)

The idea that women are in danger just by virtue of being by themselves is so ingrained that one designer created a dress that—get this—transforms into a vending machine costume so women can be "disguised" as they walk home. (Kind of like the cartoons where people would hide in bushes and you'd see the little feet underneath walking around.) So depressing, truly. For those gals who are the traveling sort, it gets even worse. Do a Google search for women traveling, and all you get are rape prevention trips!

But the truth of the matter is, more women are doing shit on their own than ever before. Women travel abroad alone, go on vacation alone, even (gasp!) eat alone. A recent census survey actually showed that 51 percent of women in the United States are living without a spouse.[1] That means most women are living alone. Independent women indeed. Now if we could only get the rest of the world to realize it!

## So... what to do?

Stop assuming that a gal sitting by herself is waiting for someone! Maybe she's just enjoying a peaceful moment. And if you like doing stuff by yourself, do it! I'm not saying don't be safe, but don't live in fear either. It's traditional bullshit that tells us we should be relying on men to accompany us everywhere. We're cool on our own—or with other women! Go travel with girlfriends. Go out to eat by yourself. Go to a bar with a group of gals, and if some jerkoff asks why you're alone, laugh in his face. Relish your independence.

# 25

# HE'S A CELEB, SHE'S A MESS

**THERE'S SOMETHING ABOUT CELEBRITY WOMEN** that we love to hate. We relish in their anguish and bask in their breakdowns. Sure, male celebs mess up every once in a while, and we chuckle. But for the most part, it's the hot mess that is young celebrity women that keeps us coming back for more. We're like a country full of enablers.

We laugh at male celebrity messes: Nick Nolte's mug shot, Billy Joel's drunk driving. But we don't react with disgust in the way we do with women. We don't call philandering male celebrities "whores" or "sluts." We don't mock them for "getting fat" or having kids. We don't wonder if they're anorexic.

Though I suppose it's not surprising—if you look at women celebrities, particularly young women, you see a microcosm of societal sexism at work. We love them when they're young, taut, and gyrating at our command. But if they slip up, or have the nerve to get older, we're right there, waiting to tear them down. (Sounds like what we do to women in general, never mind celebs!)

The epitome of this female-celeb hating, of course, is Britney Spears. Who else embodies the virgin/whore hot mess better than she does? From her cheery schoolgirl dancing to shaving her head in a stupor, she *is* the fallen public woman. Though nothing beat her final descent into being forever mocked like she was for her performance at the 2007 MTV Video Music Awards. Now, there's no doubt that it was a bad performance. She seemed to just be going through the motions, and I, probably like a lot of other people, felt bad for her. And I was absolutely livid to read the gossip mags—and even traditional news outlets—comment on how "fat" she was! Whether it was a news story saying she had a "paunch" or a cable news dude calling her chunky—it was just fucking gross and wrong. (Um, and when was the last frigging time a male musician's beer belly made news?)

One of my fave writers, Rebecca Traister, breaks it down:

> Spears has come to represent something—something important enough that it keeps rearing its head. As has been pointed out before, she embodies the disdain in which this culture holds its young women: the desire to sexualize and spoil them while young, and to degrade and punish them as they get older.[1]

But *why* exactly are stories about famous women's demise so much more appealing than news about a man's downfall? Especially considering that so many of the people reading and laughing at the likes of Paris, Lindsay, and Britney are women themselves! Is it because we have so little control in our own lives that taking joy in others' misfortune makes us feel better? Or maybe we like seeing the young women who represent these unattainable beauty standards crashing and burning. (Kind of like when you ripped the heads off the Barbie dolls you played with so much.) We hate them but idolize them at the same time. It's fucked.

But it's also predictable—we hate/idolize women in much the same way that society does. It's a misogyny thing. After all, I don't

DOUBLE STANDARDS EVERY WOMAN SHOULD KNOW

111

think it's a coincidence that one of the favorite pastimes of celebrity photographers is trying to get a "getting out of the car" nekkid-vagina shot. Look, they're women, and they're whores!

Robert Thompson, a professor of popular culture at Syracuse University in New York, was quoted in an article about celeb girls gone bad as saying, "We have had years of young male stars running amok. It is now so much more fun for the public to see beautiful young women being hauled off to jail."[2] That reminds me of a quote from Edgar Allan Poe, who said, "The death of a beautiful woman is unquestionably the most poetical topic in the world." And it really is true. The destruction of a young woman is the oldest, most popular story in the book. And now it's being lived out in front of us day after day. Modern-day girl celebs are the traditional damsels in distress, but instead of trying to save them, we're cheering for them to trip up.

And this isn't just about bad karma and being gossipy. It isn't about letting male celebs off the hook. It's about bashing other women because we hate ourselves. It's about idolizing women who are train wrecks. And it's got to stop.

# So... what to do?

Stop the schadenfreude! Taking pleasure in someone else's pain seems to be an American (or worldwide, I suppose) pastime, but when it comes to young women in the spotlight, we've gone too far. When are we going to realize that hating other women—no matter how much money they have or how far they've fallen—is just as bad for ourselves as it is for anyone else? And that by buying into the media frenzy surrounding young women falling into disrepair, we're buying into a culture that would be just as happy to see any woman—including you—trip and fall.

# 26

# ♦ HE'S HUSKY,
## SHE'S INVISIBLE

**WHERE, OH WHERE, ARE THE WOMEN OF SIZE?** The women we see on television and in the movies are all small, skinny, and svelte. And while there are male actors of all shapes and sizes represented on television and in the movies, the only women with a dress size in the double digits we see are those who play the "fat" character! "Normal" women, it seems, are all tiny (besides the boobs, of course. Got to have The Boobs).

Think about all the heavier male actors you can name: Paul Giamatti, Jack Black, and James Gandolfini are a few. Or if you're into old-school comedy, actors like John Candy, John Belushi, and Chris Farley were popular back in the day. Now, what about actresses of size? Drawing a blank? That's because outside of a handful of women (who are usually recruited to play a character whose size will be an issue in the plot), big women are pretty much invisible in the media and entertainment biz.

Yes, movies will *occasionally* take on issues of size, but rarely in a way that's flattering. Consider the 2001 movie *Shallow Hal* with Jack Black and Gwyneth Paltrow. The movie seems to have a positive message: The main character falls in love with an overweight woman because he's been hypnotized to see her inner beauty. After some trials and tribulations, he wants to be with her even without being hypnotized because, he's fallen in love with her as a person. All very charming, but the movie still presupposes that a man needs to be convinced to

JESSICA VALENTI

love a woman of a certain size and that she wouldn't be able to get some loving otherwise. As if someone just couldn't be attracted to her (gasp!) appearance. Also problematic—though common—is that the love interest isn't played by an actual woman who is larger, but by an actress in a "fat suit."

Marisa Meltzer at *Bitch* magazine says the fat suit is "the new minstrel show." Not only does it have a long history ("Wanna make a funny movie? It's a pretty easy formula: Zip a skinny actor into a latex suit. Watch her/him eat, walk, and try to find love. Hilarity will ensue"), but it also perpetuates some fairly gross stereotypes:

> Fat Monica [from the TV show *Friends*] really takes the proverbial cake. She dresses badly, has no self-control, eats junk food, has poor hygiene, and is a virgin. She's the opposite of the control-freak Thin Monica, who has the husband, the job, and the adoring friends.[1]

Fat people are one of the last groups of folks whom it's totally acceptable to mock in public. You know, because it's for their own good—'cause of the "obesity crisis" or something. Please. You know, I've always been lucky to be a size deemed acceptable by society. But my freshman year of college, which proved to be depressing for many other reasons (I won't get into that!), I gained about twenty pounds. I didn't really notice, truth be told, because I had always had the privilege of never having to pay attention to my size. But when I went home that summer, some of my relatives were all too pleased to tell me how fat I had gotten. Or how I looked like I had a "beer belly." I lost the weight in a couple of months, but just the handful of comments I got stayed with me for a long time. Which is why this next trope in movies about fat women is just hilarious.

A common theme in movies that feature women of size is the poor mocked girl who is just too nice and innocent to realize people are making fun of her. Kate Harding, who blogs about fat-acceptance issues at Shapely Prose, notes:

> By the time I was eight years old, all the very special episodes and TV movies based on this ludicrous premise—fat chick gets nominated for Homecoming/Prom Queen and/or asked to The Big Dance by The Big Man on Campus, and somehow fails to see anything wrong with this picture—sent me through the goddamned roof. Have the people who write this shit ever actually MET a fat person? And hell, even if they haven't, can they seriously think it's possible for anyone to go through life with people snickering behind her back and saying hateful shit to her face every single day, and not catch on to the possibility that she just might not be the most popular girl in school?[2]

Yet heavier male actors prevail. And they get parts that *don't* focus on their weight—parts that are a luxury for women actresses.

# So... what to do?

Support movies and media that portray women of all sizes. That includes magazines that claim to value women no matter what but always seem to find a size 0 to stick on their cover! Check out groups like Big Moves (www.bigmoves.org), a performance group for women "dedicated to getting more people of all sizes into the dance studio and up on stage." My friend Jaclyn Friedman is a part of the organization, and let me tell you—they do some great stuff. Visit blogs like Big Fat Deal (www.bfdblog.com) and Big Fat Blog (www.bigfatblog.com) to get the skinny (pun intended) on what's going on in the fat-acceptance movement. And don't watch movies or shows where fat people are the punch line. Boycott fat suits.

# 27

# HE'S A MAN, SHE'S A MOM

**WOMEN, IT SEEMS, ARE DEFINED BY WHETHER OR NOT** they have children. Or how *many* children they have. Or if they're an evil, childless spinster like me. (Hey, I have a dog. That's kinda like a kid.) Unlike men, who are primarily judged by their accomplishments, their profession, their personality, women are looked at for their appearance and their ability to pop out the little ones.

I definitely want kids. I want to raise droves of little feminist activists who call out playground sexism and grow up to roll their eyes at me when I talk about how things used to be so terrible for women. "Mo-om! Enough about the Hyde Amendment already—that's sooo 2007!" But I don't want my identity to be so tied up with motherhood that I'm seen not as an individual, but as so-and-so's mom. (Yeah, I have no clever imaginary kids' names; I'm not *that* eager to have children.)

But it seems that that's the only option women have today. We're not good women unless we have kids, and once we do—we're moms first, foremost, and forever.

Of course, this is why it's always women who are expected to worry about "balancing work and home," because motherhood is supposed to be our priority—not men's. And, yes, I know about the arguments that women are just naturally more inclined to be caregivers because of the whole carrying-a-baby-and-giving-birth thing. But I say once they're out, they're out. Why should the onus of caring for a kid fall so heavily on women while men get off scot-free?

And I truly believe that because women have been relegated to this bizarre world where motherhood defines what kind of person we are, we've started to go nuts. Women who have become über-competitive with their children, or with how good a mother they are, are acting out (in my humble opinion) because they're not supposed to be competitive in the workplace or anywhere outside the home. This is their new domain. Take, for example, a report from NPR about affluent women who are having more and more children as a way to transfer their competitive energy—they call it "competitive birthing."[1] She who has the most kids wins. Seems like one of those sketchy trend pieces, but I don't think it's that unbelievable. As Feministing blogger Ann Friedman said about the story, "[I]t doesn't seem completely far-fetched to me that women who used to be career-driven would want to direct their competitive energies somewhere—and for some women, that's become a quest to be the best mom."

But this isn't just about the ability to work and raise a family, or how women are expected to do more in the domestic sphere. This is about the very pervasive—and troubling—myth that being a woman means having children. That we're not "whole" without them.

If men choose not to have children, no one will be aghast at them or tell them they'll change their mind. When they go to get a vasectomy, no one refuses them. (I've heard many stories of women being turned away when they try to get their tubes tied.) Women, on the other hand, are expected to want children. Oodles of them. So when a woman says she doesn't want kids, the assumption is that she's going through a phase, or that there's something wrong with her—or that she's just plain selfish. After all, it's a woman's job to have the babies!

But the truth is, more and more women are opting out of parenthood. The U.S. Census reports that women in their twenties to fifties who don't have children have been growing at fast rates over the last ten years. And a report from the National Marriage Project at Rutgers University says that nearly one out of five women in their early forties is childless—thirty years ago it was one out of ten.[2] And despite what media frenzies tell you about poor career women desperately trying to get pregnant after spending fruitless years developing their high-powered professions, most women who are childless are completely comfortable with the idea.

In fact, a 2007 study says that women are much more comfortable with the idea of childlessness than men are. The research, which was published in *The Journal of Marriage and Family,* shows that the results may be due to the fact that men experience "strong economic and social rewards" for being fathers, while women experience more pressure and demands on their day-to-day lives.[3] Despite stereotypes that assume women care more about having children than men do, this study says that it's actually women who understand more about the *costs* of having children. Nadine Kaslow, chief psychologist at Emory medical school in Atlanta, said the findings of the report show "women who are successful professionals make a choice that they don't want to have children in their lives, because they have other things in their lives." Men, however, "tend to think that is what you do in life. You grow up and have a baby." So why try to conflate women's identity with whether or not they have kids? Well, once again, it benefits a society that lives on sexism. If we're not "real" women unless we have babies (and stay home to take care of them, of course), then women are going to feel pressure to adhere to traditional gender roles.

Don't have babies, ever. Just kidding. Have babies, don't have babies, raise Sea Monkeys for all I care. Just don't let anyone ever tell you that who you are as a person has anything to do with the personal family choices you make.

# 28

# HE'S DATING A YOUNGER WOMAN,

## SHE'S A COUGAR

**CAN SOMEONE PLEASE TELL ME WHY IT IS THAT** it's perfectly normal for a man to date someone who looks like she could be his granddaughter, but if a woman dates a younger man she's a cougar? Or an oddity? And I swear I'm not just saying this because I'm dating a younger man. (Well, maybe a little.)

It's no great secret that older men frequently date younger women. It's not frowned upon, really—it's actually exalted more than anything. After all, they don't call them "trophy" wives for nothing! Think Donald Trump, Hugh Hefner (eew! On second thought, *don't* think about him), or any other old guy with a young woman. While you and I may take a look at their relationships and cringe a little, the fact remains that society supports them. But an older woman with a younger man? It's treated as a novelty, a joke, or a premise for bad porn. But the fact is, more and more older women *are* dating below their age.

A 2003 AARP study showed that 34 percent of women over forty were dating younger men, and 35 percent preferred it to dating older men. Another recent study found that in more recent years, only 25 percent of brides have been younger than their grooms.[1]

While my boyfriend is a mere five years my junior, I still get a lot more comments on the relationship than you would expect. Guy friends joke with me about "robbing the cradle." Family members look on in concern, wondering if a younger man will be able to get serious with me (translation: want to get married). I've even had someone wonder aloud if I was with my boyfriend because I wanted to be with a younger man I could "control." (Anyone who knows me knows that I like men of any age whom I can control, but that's beside the point!) It can't just be that we're two people who like each other a lot. There has to be something more to it.

Now, I've heard all sorts of reasons why it's more "normal" for older men to date younger women, and not vice versa. That it's because of money. (Well, women have more money than ever.) That it's biology—men want to spread their seed and be with women young enough to have babies. (Sorry, I just don't buy it. Older men can still have babies, but recent studies show that men's sperm ages, too—and can cause birth defects. So it's not just our old-ass eggs, guys!) But I think at the end of the day, some people are uncomfortable with older women/younger men relationships because it's not the power dynamic they expect. Because, let's face it, with age comes wisdom, more money, and more power. So in a sexist society, it's understandable that older men would be with younger women—it adheres to the power dynamic already set in place by the patriarchy. (I know, I just got all women's studies on your ass. Relax, it only hurts for a second.) Men with more power, women with less. That's why it's unfathomable that a woman could do the same thing an older man does—because she's not supposed to have the power in a relationship!

And that's why it's so easy—and so necessary—to fetishize or make fun of older women being with younger men. By diminishing the validity of the relationship by making cougar jokes or watching MILF porn, men are getting that power back. And let's be serious—jokes and porn abound when it comes to this kind of couple.

Of course, the most popular incarnation of the older-woman-as-joke is the notion of cougars. Urban Dictionary defines a cougar as "an older woman who frequents clubs in order to score with a much younger man. The cougar can be anyone from an overly surgically altered wind tunnel victim, to an absolute sad and bloated old horn-meister, to a real hottie or MILF."[2] (See what I mean about taking the power back? Sigh.) What's really interesting about all the "cougar" web-sites that have cropped up is that many of the women featured are in their late twenties—as if that's old! I guess in porno-land it's over the hill, but come on now.

Or there's the prevalence of MILF (please don't make me spell it out) porn. Most of this stuff is about men finding older women (one site is call MILF Hunter, for example) to have sex with. It's not always about men in power, but the simple act of sexualizing a relationship and fetishizing is a way to make it less valid, less important.

So now, instead of being in a relationship where you're dating a younger man who makes you feel independent and loved, you have to feel like the butt of someone's joke or the star of someone's fantasy.

# So... what to do?

Keep on keeping on, ladies! Date those younger men if that's what you want. And don't let anyone call you a cougar. Ick. And don't forget that older women can date younger men, because we *have* power. Susan Winter, who's in her fifties and is the coauthor of *Older Women, Younger Men: New Options for Love and Romance*, says, "When women as a group are able to have their own economic and social standing and have a power base, they are now able to pick the man that they want rather than having to choose the man to support them and give them social status. . . . Now we have choices." Indeed.

# 29

# HE'S DRUNK, SHE'S A VICTIM

**WHOEVER THOUGHT THERE WOULD BE AN INEBRIATION** double standard?! But indeed there is. And unfortunately, it's not even funny—it's dangerous.

Men are supposed to get drunk to bond and to have fun. At worst, someone ends up waking up with an unfortunately placed tattoo or with a fun story about ending up in Mexico or some such shit. If you're a woman, you're supposed to drink to "loosen up," specifically for the sex. And while I'm definitely not against having some drinks and getting your sex on, this dynamic is part of what makes for date and acquaintance rape—and that's just scary.

I have done my fair share of partying. You might even say that for a time I was a party girl. I went out and got drunk, fell down while drunk, and definitely let alcohol grease the wheels for several hookups. But I also saw some disturbing shit in those days that I wish I hadn't. I saw girlfriends the morning after a night of binge drinking who said they didn't remember if they had had sex. I saw guys grabbing at women in a way that went beyond sexual or flirty—it was aggressive. I saw stuff that I'd rather not even mention here. Again, this isn't to say that I think drinking is an inherently bad thing. But I do think that our drinking culture and the inebriation double standard target women in a creepy way, and that they allow for women to be blamed when something bad happens.

Take cheap drinks and bar deals. The ladies'-night phenomenon is really something else—you have to love the genius of bar owners who make it easy and cheap for women to get ridiculously drunk, and then have guys pay to come and hang out with them. Be honest—you know this shit isn't about making a nice night for women; it's about providing drunk women for men! (Besides, the drinks at ladies' night are always watered down or sucky sugary margaritas that give you a wicked headache in the morning.)

But it's not just crappy bar deals we're talking about. Just think about the way that women are still (still!) blamed for their own rapes if they had the gall to have a drink or two. The common sentiment is still that women who get drunk either are sluts who are looking for an excuse to have sex or should have known better than to make themselves "vulnerable." Writer (and general badass lady) Jaclyn Friedman wrote an amazing article on drinking and rape in which she discussed her own assault and what could have been done to stop it:

> Let's look a little more closely at that correlation between rape and alcohol. That's not a correlation between female drinking and rape. It's a correlation between all drinking and rape. In fact, studies have shown that it's more likely that a male rapist has been drinking than that his female victim has. So if we want to raise awareness about the links between drinking and rape, we should start by getting the word out to men that alcohol is likely to impair their ability to respond appropriately if a sexual partner says "no." When was the last time you read that article in any kind of publication?[1]

Well, because of the drinking (or any kind of substance, really) double standard, you never would hear of something like that. Instead, the onus for rape is put on the woman who was drinking, not the rapist—drunk or not. Jaclyn hit the nail on the head: "The silence around men's drinking is, of course, part of a much larger 'boys will be boys' culture, one which played a large part in my assault. The party I attended was for a men's sports team; the coaches provided the alcohol." So why is it, then, that all of the warnings about rape and drinking are directed at women? Shouldn't we be telling young men that drinking puts them in danger of crossing the line? No way—because guys' drinking is fun; it's normal socializing. But girls' drinking has always meant the same thing: sex.

Take the seventeen-year-old woman in California who was gang-raped—despite three female eyewitnesses pushing their way into a room where the girl, with clothes around her ankles and vomit on her face, was being assaulted with ten men looking on. (The three young women fought to get her out of the room; they had seen her being dragged in and figured something bad was going on.) Charges against the men were dropped—apparently they couldn't know if the woman consented or not because she was drunk. Never mind that she had puke all over her—that sure screams, "I'm ready to have sex," huh? (And just a thought—if a guy woke up and had been raped by another man after drinking too much, do you have any doubt in your mind that people would believe the victim? Just saying.)

Now, you can't talk drinking, assault, and woman blaming without talking about Girls Gone Wild. Tricking drunk women, or making out like coerced drunk women are just being the exhibitionists they always wanted to be, is the whole philosophy behind the porn (and sleaze) empire Girls Gone Wild. I mean, in what universe can you sign a consent form while shitfaced? If you signed a will or a contract while under the influence of something, it wouldn't be valid. Yet drunken teens agreeing to strip? Not a problem. And again, I'm not saying that all the women in those videos have been taken advantage of. But the model that GGW is working under assumes that these women need to be tricked, convinced, and, most important—good and drunk. I'm sorry, but that just does not sound like fun.

## So... what to do?

Don't get trashed. Obviously, I'm not against drinking. And I don't think that women should forgo having a social life in what will probably be a vain attempt to protect themselves against assault. (Remember, it's not a drunk woman who facilitates a rape, it's the fucking rapist.) But I do think that young women drink too much and that it's just generally bad for us. Besides, nothing worth doing is more fun when you're drunk. Arm yourself with knowledge about rape culture and victim blaming. And if you have a bad feeling at a party, or about a drunk friend or a drunk guy, follow your instincts.

# 30

# ♦ HE'S STOIC,
## ♦ SHE'S FRIGID

**WHEN MEN ARE QUIET, THEY'RE MYSTERIOUS.** When they're a little sullen, they're James Dean deep. When women are serious or quiet (or not constantly chipper, at least), we're cold bitches. We're frigid. We're snobs.

I am a *very* gregarious person. I talk loud, I crack jokes. I like being in big groups of people. My sister, Vanessa, however . . . isn't. She's just as funny and friendly, but she's more reserved. I remember when we were teens, she would complain that everyone assumed she was a bitch or snotty because she didn't open up right away. I always found it unfair.

Now, while the ability to be a quiet or serious person without being labeled cold may not seem like it should be a top feminist priority, it's actually coming from a pretty interesting place. My least favorite form of street harassment is when a guy asks why I'm not smiling. It's related to that: Women aren't allowed to be quiet or stoic or shy—or, hell, just in a bad mood—without being criticized. Women are bitchy and frigid if we don't seem accessible at all times, for the most part to men. We're supposed to be perpetually friendly. Who wants to live up to that? And seriously, when was the last time you heard a quiet woman described as "deep"?

Men who are serious are just that—serious. Think laconic cowboys and Clint Eastwood–style movie heroes. Strong and silent is a desirable personality trait for men—women, not so much. Because where silence in men is seen as strength, silence in women (if not seen as bitchy) is seen as weakness—she's shy, a wallflower.

And, of course, the sexual aspect of this double standard is hard to miss as well. If we're not being "friendly," then we're supposedly not as open to sexual attention. (The horror!) I recall being at this awful bar in college called the Post—any SUNY Albany alumns out there know the place I'm talking about—where one night there was an impromptu wet T-shirt contest. (Hey, I never said I went to classy joints!) I was kind of horrified by the whole thing—the way the guys were crowding the women involved, the things they were yelling ("Take it off, slut!" and the like), and how the atmosphere in the room changed from jovial to . . . well, a little scary. I left the bar, only to take shit from my guy friends later—I was being too "serious," I was a killjoy. Now, like I've said before, I was a bit of party girl and always was down to have a good time. But the minute I was uncomfortable and didn't want to be a part of something that was supposed to be "fun," I was labeled as unable to have a good time. It's just too bad that "fun" always seems to involve women as entertainment.

I also think that there are shades of misogyny in this double standard—I mean, perhaps the reason that a serious, quiet woman isn't liked much is that she has power. If women are happy and chipper and laughing all the time, then men don't have to take us as seriously. If we're quiet, or thoughtful, then men have to think of us in a serious way—as more than just entertainment value. But that's just one gal's opinion.

But take the reactions to Senator Hillary Clinton's presidential run, for example. How many times have you heard her described as cold, frigid, or—of course—a bitch? That's also why you'll hear male pundits talk about Clinton's voice as "shrill" or "grating." There's nothing that annoys men like the sound of a woman in power! I think this has a tremendous amount to do with her being a serious woman. In fact, I think that some men (I'm talking to you, Chris Matthews!) are so freaked out by the idea of a serious woman with influence that they're almost amazed that such women exist. (I'm thinking back to when MSNBC's Matthews asked Senator Chris Dodd, "Do you find it difficult to debate a woman?")

## So... what to do?

Well, for the first time ever, I'm not going to tell you to "speak up"! We should be able to be quiet, reserved, serious, and even "no fun" if we want. We need to be able to turn our backs on the idea that a woman's job is to provide permanent fun and entertainment for the men in our lives (or in public spaces). It's time that we enjoyed our silence.

# 31

# ♀ HE'S COVERED,
## SHE'S SCREWED

**DID YOU KNOW THAT AS RECENTLY AS 2005,** rapists were getting their Viagra covered by Medicaid but rape victims across the country couldn't get emergency contraception? Apparently, choosing to not get pregnant through rape was just much more controversial than paying for a sex offender's hard-on. Sit on that for a while. Sure, it's an extreme example, but it highlights the ridiculous disparity between the sexes when it comes to health and medical care. Men are covered, women are fucked.

The truth is, women have been getting the short end of the health-care stick for a long time—mostly because men have been used as the standard of care. Let me elaborate: When doctors and scientists did research on things like heart attacks and cancer, they used male subjects in their studies. This meant that all the information they got about symptoms, how to treat patients, and so on, really related only to men. That's why certain diseases go underdiagnosed in women—and it's killing us. In fact, three million women potentially have heart disease that has gone undetected because the signs and symptoms are different for women than for men. This situation is even more dire for women of color, who are often ignored altogether.

Another issue with women and health is that women require a lot more preventative care than men do—which isn't always covered by insurance and isn't always recommended to women. For example, women need regular Pap smears, mammograms, and osteoporosis tests—all preventative.

But for some reason or another (cough, sexism, cough) women's health is often given the shaft by the government. Whether it's targeting women because of reproductive-justice issues like abortion and birth control, or just plain being greedy, women in the United States are struggling. In fact, there are sixteen million uninsured women in the United States (I'm one of them, in fact). That's insane. And let me tell you, a lot of folks just don't care.

In 2007, conservatives and the religious right opposed legislation that would renew and expand funding for the State Children's Health Insurance Program (SCHIP). Now, this is a program to provide for kids, but the reason that the conservatives were all bent out of shape was that it helped out pregnant women. For real. You see, Democrats removed some anti-choice amendments that had the nerve to identify women as the beneficiaries of care while they're pregnant. Anti-choice conservative assholes on the Family Research Council released a statement saying:

> The new House bill changes the SCHIP program to cover health insurance for a "pregnant woman" rather than cover the child in the womb. This would undermine the "unborn child rule" and could possibly allow funding for abortions in those States that include abortion as part of their Medicaid health coverage for pregnant women.

What they were really pissed about was the language change: Pregnant women shouldn't benefit, unborn children should. But this actually gets to the heart of the matter ... a lot of this is about hating women, and hating us because we have The Sex. Seriously.

That's why they don't want to repeal the Hyde Amendment—which maintains that Medicaid can't pay for abortions. (It's nice to punish low-income women!) That's why they don't care that birth control prices are soaring on college campuses. That's why it's cool with them that abstinence education—which has been proven dangerous, especially to women—gets funding despite its ineffectiveness. Shit, they'd rather that women get cancer—*cancer*—than allow for the HPV vaccine to be legal.

Before the HPV vaccine was approved by the FDA, a lot of folks were fighting tooth and nail to make sure that it wouldn't be. Why? Because it would make girls slutty. Just like they said emergency contraception would! (The logic was that if you gave preteen girls a shot that made sure they wouldn't get HPV, they would see it as a chance to go whore around. You know, just like how when you get a flu shot you go around looking for people to sneeze on you.) Never mind that 25 percent of women in America become infected with HPV, the STD that causes cervical cancer. More important to keep girls "pure."

They don't care about our health, gals. They just don't. They do, however, care *very* much what we do with our na-nas.

Think of all the legislation concerning women's health that conservatives put forward: Most of it is about limiting our access to birth control and abortion, and making sure that we have as many babies as possible—if we're white. If we're not white, it's about making sure we have no babies, ever.

Kind of interesting that a country that cares so little about whether we're insured, whether we're being treated correctly, and whether we have the care that we need would care *so* much about whether or not we get laid. But so it is.

So... *what to do?*

Make sure you're informed about women's healthcare, particularly preventative health. Check out organizations like SisterSong that fight for women's health. Keep abreast of reproductive health and justice issues—because that's where they're hitting us the hardest. And get your ass to a doctor on a regular basis.

# 32

# HE'S REPRESENTED,

## SHE'S A TOKEN

**IN THE 1990S, WAL-MART PULLED A SHIRT FROM ITS STORES** for fear that it was offensive. The "controversial" shirt featured a picture of Margaret—a character from the comic strip *Dennis the Menace*—saying, "Someday a woman will be president." This is what they found so horrifying that it was removed from stores. I think that tells you a little something about where we are with women and politics.

Perhaps no double standard between men and women is more in the public eye than the gender gap in politics. In the United States right now, women hold only 16 percent of the seats in Congress—and of those women, only 24 percent are women of color. The United States falls behind dozens of other countries in terms of women's political participation. Rwanda, Sweden, Finland, and Costa Rica are the top four countries with women in Parliament—we're at number sixty-eight.[1] (Think of that number when someone is telling you how American women have nothing left to fight for and how feminism is irrelevant. Hmph.) And now that Sandra Day O'Connor has retired, Justice Ruth Bader Ginsburg is the *only* woman left on the Supreme Court of the United States.

When it comes to positions of power, women just don't have it. We're given scraps here and there, but for the most part, women are tokenized. Just take a look at Secretary of State Condoleezza Rice—she's the person most often cited when you start to talk about racism or sexism in politics. But she's a black woman and she's up there, so it all must be good, right? Not so much. Just because one woman, one person of color, one anyone, is put in a position of power, it hardly means that racism or sexism or classism doesn't exist. It means someone threw us a bone.

That said, we are doing better than we have been . . . well, ever. The elections in 2006 had some huge wins for women. Dems took control of the House, and Nancy Pelosi became the first female Speaker of the House. While sixteen women in the Senate is still a low number, it's the highest we've ever had. Clearly, American voters are taking women politicians seriously. But the same can't be said for others. After the 2006 election, there was a lot of sexism-based resentment that can be described only as a "girls are icky" line of argument (whining). During MSNBC's election coverage, Chris Matthews said that Senator Clinton gave a "barn-burner speech, which is harder to give for a woman; it can grate on some men when they listen to it—fingernails on a blackboard." He also said that Pelosi will "have to do the good fight with the president over issues" and asked: "How does she do it without screaming? How does she do it without becoming grating?" Nothing like the sound of an uppity woman, huh, Chris?

But the best dig came from President Bush himself, who said of Pelosi, "[I]n my first act of bipartisan outreach since the election, I shared with her the names of some Republican interior decorators who can help her pick out the new drapes in her new offices." Of course, taking sexist swipes at women is nothing new. But it seems that the higher in political rank women climb, the bigger babies some men become. (So grow up, boys. We're not going anywhere.)

As I write this, someone is running who may very well become the first woman president of the United States. And while I'm not going to say who I'm supporting in the race, I have to admit that a woman winning the presidency would be amazing. And long fucking overdue.

# So... what to do?

Vote. Seriously, you'd better. Younger women's voices matter and can make a huge impact on elections. So get your ass out there. If you know a young woman who should run for public office (or if you should!), encourage her to get out there. The biggest reason women cite for *not* running is that they think they're not qualified. Men who have the same qualifications, by the way, never think that they're unqualified. Help to put an end to the idea that women don't belong in politics. When you hear a sexist asshole like Chris Matthews say something vile, call in to let them know so. Same goes for your friends. Fighting those stereotypes starts at home, too.

# 33

# ♀ HE'S NEAT,
## SHE'S NEUROTIC

**WOMEN, IT SEEMS, HAVE A SPECIAL RELATIONSHIP** with dirt and cleanliness. Again, because of the vagina and all, we're supposed to have an innate ability to clean a room like nobody's business. We love it. It's what we were born to do. Men, on the other hand, are filthy, nasty creatures who would probably live in their own shit if women weren't there to tell them what to do.

Or at least that's what we're supposed to believe. (I'm convinced it's all a clever scheme to keep women doing laundry for the next hundred or so years, but that's beside the point.)

Women are still doing the bulk of domestic labor—cooking, cleaning, taking care of the kiddos, and so on. But it's the cleaning that's killing us. Dishes, dusting, vacuuming, toilet cleaning. Just . . . ugh. According to a 2002 study by the University of Michigan Institute for Social Research, American men do sixteen hours of housework a week, while women do twenty-seven.[1] An even more recent study showed that married women do more housework than single or cohabiting women—apparently the act of getting married makes you all housewifey or something. (Single women do the least housework of all—just something to think about.) And according the Department of Labor, because of all the housework women are doing, they have significantly less leisure time than men do. So clearly, things are not all equal at home. And frankly, a lot of people would like to keep it that way.

Women doing the majority of housework and domestic labor—and not being happy about it—is one of those things that bring out some of the funniest anti-woman theories. The argument that women are just naturally more inclined to clean because we can't stand dirtiness (clearly *someone* has never seen my place) and men don't mind is the most common. And, of course, it comes from predictable places. Take, for example, anti-feminist blog Angry Harry:

> The reason that men do less housework than women is because, quite simply, they are less easily offended by any given level of mess. . . . Men just do not respond to the same low levels of untidiness as do women. And so whenever the female threshold is reached, and the good woman must whisk herself away to tackle the debris around the house, the man remains undisturbed, at peace, and contented with his surroundings.[2]

Angry Harry also has some interesting theories on why men don't like housework:

> If God had wanted men to do housework then he would have genetically programmed women to drool over men while they did it. . . . The sight of men doing the dishes would have made their G-spots zizz. . . . A woman who wants her man to do housework is unconsciously seeking a divorce. She has no feeling for him—as a man, that is.

Charming! But when the argument that women just don't like dirt (and men do?) doesn't work, the powers that be pull out some doozies.

Like when *The Washington Post* ran an article headlined "Women's Liberation Through Housework." Seriously. And this was in 2007, not 1957. Reporter Rena Corey argued that she gets tremendous satisfaction out of keeping a clean home, her "little kingdom."[3] That's all well and good, but what in the world does that have to do with women's "liberation"? Feministing blogger Ann Friedman responded better than I ever could:

> Rena might be satisfied to spend her adult life as the happy homemaker, but the vast majority of us are not. See, those of us who manage to part with our Swiffers long enough to venture outside for a paycheck know that, as Rena notes, there are indeed minute-to-minute unpleasant tasks in the work world. But they add up to a lot more than a sparkling toilet. They allow women to have influence in the public sphere—the world beyond the "little kingdom," where important decisions are made about the direction of society, and where money and power change hands.[4]

And that's the point, really. If we're more focused on housework and how clean our little kingdoms are, then we won't be in the public sphere making decisions that affect the world, not just our apartments.

That's why I don't think it's any small coincidence that there has been a bevy of recent articles touting women doing housework. And the way they're pushing it is hilarious. Take this headline from the BBC: "Housework cuts breast cancer risk."[5] Okay, then. What the results of the study *actually* showed was that moderate, regular forms of exercise are effective in cutting cancer risks. But instead of pushing that, the media jumped on the dusting angle. Another headline says, "Women prefer housekeeping to love." Yet another says that married men will earn more money if their wives do the household chores. ("Clean that floor, honey—my salary depends on it!")

So... what to do?

There's a reason they're pushing the idea that women love to clean and men don't. In our happy little sexist world, things run much better when women are relegated to the home. It's even better when we believe that we *want* to be there. So don't believe this nonsense. Better that your house goes undusted for a couple of weeks so you can make a difference somewhere other than your kitchen.

# ✦ HE'S FUN,
## SHE'S FRIVOLOUS

**SHOPPING IS VAIN.** Reading celebrity weeklies is for dummies. Lifetime? For losers. Watching sports and reading lad mags, however, is manly and fun. Golf is relaxing.

When it comes to hobbies or having fun, men's interests are valid and women's are frivolous.

Now, I'm not a fan of stereotyping certain behavior as female—assuming that all women shop or that men don't, for example. But there's no denying that particular activities are associated with specific genders, and that the ones associated with women are pretty readily dismissed—or straight-up hated.

Men watching sports is considered manly, and it's a hobby! Same thing with hunting or reading *Playboy* or doing other "masculine" things. It's *cool* when a guy plays poker with his friends.

But women shopping? Clearly vapid. Women's magazines? Ridiculous. Never mind that certain things—like shopping or paying attention to our looks—are demanded of us by society. So if we go shopping or get expensive haircuts, we're shallow. But if we don't, we're not "taking care" of ourselves or we're ugly or lazy.

Just think about how much hostility and mocking is directed at "women's programming" like Oxygen or Lifetime (shit, even I make fun of them). Or how shows like *Bridezillas* make fun of women for how shallow and obsessed they are over weddings—of course, that's yet *another* thing we're taught that we must care about. We just can't win.

Then, of course, there's hell to pay if men dare debase themselves by doing anything considered feminine. Conservative writer and wannabe pundit Debbie Schlussel, for example, devoted an entire blog post to how horrible it was that men would take up knitting. For real. (To give you some perspective, this is also a woman who said that any gal who gets a tattoo must be a whore, because "a woman who doesn't take long to agree to repeatedly put a needle in her body generally doesn't take long before she acquiesces to putting other things into her body.")

> In my ongoing examination of our society's largely successful attempt to feminize America's men (and masculinize the women), I've been watching the growing trend of knitting for boys and men. . . . The latest point on this downward decline of masculinity is the book *Knitting with Balls: A Hands-On Guide to Knitting for the Modern Man.*
>
> . . . One of my hometown newspapers raved about it over the weekend. I'm guessing the woman who wrote the review also likes her son to figure skate and is sending him to flight attendant school next. . . . If you're a scientist in a remote Antarctic camp of all men studying the extreme cold and you need a new scarf or hat, then knitting is okay. But, other than that, if you're a guy, don't scratch that itch. Knitting ain't very manly.[1]

Get that, guys? You should be off playing football or killing something, not doing "girlie" stuff. I mean, who in the world would want to be . . . feminine?

And that's really the point. At the end of the day, when interests that are considered female are thought of as frivolous, *women themselves* are seen as frivolous. It's *women* who are silly, *women* who are frivolous and not to be taken seriously. And that's where the danger in this double standard lies.

# So... what to do?

Of course, not all women like the same things. And it's bad enough that women are stereotyped as constashoppers with no interests outside of looking good and getting married. But the fact is, as long as we mock things that are considered inherently female, we're mocking ourselves. We're buying into the notion that the things women like are stupid just by virtue of being feminine. Which is an insult to all women. So enough with mocking Lifetime (sigh) and calling women shallow. Enough with letting guys off the hook for their frivolous hobbies—golf isn't serious! Let's have fun and stop apologizing for it.

# 35

# HE WALKS FREELY,
## SHE GETS HARASSED

**IT MUST BE NICE TO WALK AROUND THE STREETS** every day without being leered at, hit on, whistled at, or shouted about. But I wouldn't know anything about that—because I have a vagina. (Apparently, owning a vagina means that you have the pleasure of perfect strangers being able to say anything they want to you. Awesome!)

Men can walk the streets freely and without being bothered, and they don't even realize it's a luxury. Women, on the other hand, have to steel themselves daily for whatever comments may come their way. Seriously—it's not a fun way to be.

And while I've heard the argument that street harassment is actually a compliment—you know, because we're supposed to be *flattered* that strange men are screaming at us about our asses—it's really a super-insidious form of sexism. Because not only do perfect strangers think that it's appropriate to be sexual toward any woman they want, but street harassment is also predicated on the idea that you're allowed to say anything to women that you want—anytime, anywhere.

That's why the harassment that annoys me the most is the kind that's not overtly sexual. My biggest pet peeve? When a random guy on the street asks me, "Why aren't you smiling?" The assumption is that (a)

because I'm a woman, I should be happy and smiling and accommodating looking at all times, and (b) he has the right to comment on my
mood. I find it *infuriating*, which is why I usually respond, "Because assholes like you make it impossible for me to walk to the subway in peace."
But I digress.

Street harassment is a big deal not just because it's fucking annoying, but also because it infringes upon the most basic right there
is—the right to just *be*. To be left alone. To be in a public space without
being bothered. I mean, is that so much to ask for?

Apparently it is. Because the solutions that some cities are offering—taking women out of public spaces—completely miss the point.
In Tokyo, 64 percent of women in their twenties and thirties reported
being groped on the train or in transit stations.[1] Instead of targeting
the harassers, the city decided to make a separate train car for women.
So did Rio de Janeiro, Moscow, and Cairo. Italy has even established a
women-only beach for the same reason. I wrote about this trend in an
article for the *Guardian*:

> There's no doubt that . . . the idea of a safe space is compel-
> ling. This international trend—which often comes couched
> in paternalistic rhetoric about "protecting" women—raises
> questions of just how equal the sexes are if women's safety
> relies on us being separated. After all, shouldn't we be tar-
> geting the gropers and harassers? The onus should be on
> men to stop harassing women, not on women to escape
> them. . . . Betsy Eudey, director of gender studies at California
> State University, says that while some single-sex environ-
> ments could be beneficial—locker rooms where people are
> expected to be naked are an obvious example—she finds that

"segregated spaces only enhance division by sex, and prevent the necessary actions needed to make public spaces safe and welcoming to all."

Who knows if that can happen, though; sexism has it so ingrained in men's minds (and even our own, sometimes) that women are there to be looked at, commented on, and grabbed that it's hard to imagine anything that would facilitate real change.

# So... what to do?

Fortunately, there are things we can do about this one. Myself, I like to call out street harassers on their bullshit (if it's not a desolate street and I feel safe). I ask them if they would talk that way to their mother or their sister. I ask them if they think it's okay to disrespect women. Or sometimes (okay, most times) I just give them the finger. There are also great websites like Hollaback that encourage women to take pictures of their harassers with their camera phones and send them in to the blog with the harassment story. (Their tagline is, "If you can't slap 'em, smack 'em!") Make those fuckers public knowledge!

And men, please, for the love of all that is good and awesome, keep it to yourself. You want to talk to a woman you see on the street? Fine— approach her and *ask* if you can speak with her. If she says no, listen to her. Walk away. It's really not that difficult.

Oh, and to the guy who yelled at me on the street when I was fifteen and told me he wanted to eat his dinner off my ass? Fuck you, pervy.

# 36

# HE'S A PORN WATCHER,
## SHE'S THE SHOW

**WE ALREADY KNOW THERE'S A DOUBLE STANDARD** when it comes to having sex. But what about *watching* sex?

Pornography is everywhere, and mainstream culture is becoming increasingly "pornified." (I'm talking to you, Pussycat Dolls!) But when it comes to porn, is women's place only in front of the camera? Are we just the objects?

I hate to say this, because as a feminist I know once you say something bad about porn, you're forever labeled anti-sex, but as it stands now, I think we are just the objects. Or at least that's what the porn industry would like us to be. Yes, there is feminist porn out there. Shit, I have friends who make it. But, like it or not, the *mainstream* porn culture is increasingly male-centric (in terms of who the audience is) and increasingly misogynistic.

Men are porn watchers, and we're the show. Now, that's a double standard if I ever heard one. We're sex embodied.

What scares me about porn now is the way it's shaping men's views on women. (As if misogyny isn't already bad enough!) And yes, there's always been pornography and there always will be. But the mainstreaming of it—and the *kind* of porn that's becoming popular—is just way too disturbing.

Robert Jensen's book *Getting Off: Pornography and the End of Masculinity* explores current porn culture in detail—something that's a lot less glamorous than what's often presented in the media. I don't have the stomach to type out some of the porn scenes that Jensen relays, but suffice it to say—they're horrible. They're about women being humiliated sexually, being treated violently, and having that be normalized. Jensen asks the obvious question:

> If pornography is increasingly cruel and degrading, why is it increasingly commonplace instead of more marginalized? How do we explain the simultaneous appearance of more, and increasingly more intense, ways to humiliate women sexually and the rising popularity of the films that present those activities?

It's scary to think that misogyny could be on an upswing, but if you take a close look at popular porn, that's exactly the message you'll get. And while there are no comprehensive studies on the effect of porn on men, I think there is some anecdotal evidence that should make all women nervous. Take, for example, eight teenage boys in Australia who were given a slap on the wrist after sexually assaulting a seventeen-year-old girl, taping the assault, and distributing it as a porn movie. They filmed the victim being forced to perform oral sex, having her hair set on fire, and being spat and urinated on. Later, the boys distributed a DVD of the attack, which they titled *Cunt, the Movie*. You can't tell me this isn't related to porn—you just can't.

Even the tamer effects of pornography—especially now that it's so easily available online—are detrimental not only to women but to men, too. I have so many male friends who are literally unable to be in a relationship because of the way that pornography has shaped how they think about women and sex. One friend described himself as "lonely," because he couldn't meet anyone who would live up to the women he watched in porn.

But this isn't to say that feminists aren't working hard to carve out female-friendly space in the sex industry. Some feminists think that rather than hurting women, sex on the Internet could actually help create a more feminist porn culture. Audacia Ray, author of *Naked on the Internet* and executive editor of *$pread,* a magazine by and for sex workers, says that "women's agency tends to be totally overlooked or ignored when it comes to the Internet, but women can use the Internet to explore their voices and their agency (sex-related and otherwise) in an unprecedented way." She goes on to say:

> Once in the industry, the Internet becomes a powerful tool for connecting with other workers on both the professional level ("How do I make a website?") and the personal level ("Who else can understand and accept the work I do?").... Most significantly, the Internet has enabled many sex workers to go independent, which means that they manage their own porn sites and escorting careers (among other professions) and do their marketing the way they want, operating without big companies, pimps, or agencies that would have claim to the cash that is rightfully theirs.

It could also mean that women can create the kind of porn that appeals to them—in which we're marketed not as objects, but as real women with real desires. Rachel Kramer Bussell, sex writer (and friend), says, "I don't think there'll ever be one correct answer to the question

'What turns women on?' and bravo for that! 'Women' are not only a massive group, but what turns an individual woman on may change over time."

So... what to do?

I'm against censorship, and I certainly don't think that we can stop the porn industry that is making so much money off of degrading women. But I do think we can support feminist porn, and encourage others *not* to watch or buy porn from film companies that make money by depicting humiliating and violent sex scenes. If you're interested in feminist or woman-centric porn, check out the Feminist Porn Awards or sex-toy shop Babes in Toyland. You can also look at Candida Royalle's Femme Productions, *Sweet Action* magazine, or Violet Blue's *The Smart Girl's Guide to Porn*.

# 37

# HE'S HOT *AND* HEADY,
## SHE'S BRAINY *OR* BOOBILICIOUS

**WHEN I WAS GROWING UP, I WAS THE SMART ONE.** I had an awkward adolescence—bad skin, ears and a nose that I had yet to grow into—but damn, did I get good grades. My sister, on the other hand, never had a zit or a bad hair day in her life and still managed to get decent grades. Bitch. (Just kidding, Vanessa!) In a family full of dark-haired Italians, Vanessa's blond hair and green eyes made her stand out. I recall an older cousin saying to me when I was around twelve years old, "Yeah, you're the smart one and your sister is the pretty one!" Let's just say that stuck with me; I was incredibly jealous of my sister from that day forward, and pissed at her for being so damned . . . pretty. (Though I'm sure that, given the fact that Vanessa is brilliant, she wouldn't have been too pleased to hear that she wasn't the "smart one.")

Of course, my sister and I weren't the only young women privy to the smart/pretty double standard: While men can be hot and smart, women don't have the luxury. We have only one of two choices: pretty or smart. You can't be both; it's too much of an anomaly, apparently.

You see the stereotype everywhere—the dorky girl in movies who becomes pretty only after a serious makeover; the hot, boobilicious girl with not a brain in her head. We're caricatures—especially when it comes to younger women.

Luckily, we're seeing more and more characters on television who defy this standard: Veronica Mars and the docs on *Grey's Anatomy,* for example. And even though a tremendous number of movies still play on the stereotype (think any movie Anna Farris has ever been in), we're making progress there, too. *Legally Blonde,* in which the main character goes from ditz to Harvard Law brainiac, and *Mean Girls,* about the cruelty of high school girls, are helping to pave the way for the idea that women can be smart and (gasp!) pretty all at the same time.

But we're still seeing the stupid/beautiful, smart/ugly model played out in "real life"—reality television and celebrity culture (okay, not *really* real life, but you know what I mean).

You need look no further than the likes of Jessica Simpson or Paris Hilton to see young women playing up the dumb angle in order to appease a public that wants nothing more from them than someone to simultaneously lust after and mock. And reality television isn't much better. You have gems like *Beauty and the Geek,* which pits smart "geeky" men against "ditzy" women. Or VH1's 2007 show *America's Most Smartest Model,* which gathers male and female models together to give them a series of tests (often humiliating) to figure out how smart they are. The men, who are of course depicted as more intelligent, are rarely commented on or made fun of in the same way the "dumb" women models are.

But you don't even have to look at trash TV to see this double standard play out. When Katie Couric was hired by CBS frat-boy pundit Joe

Scarborough, MSNBC's *Morning Joe* featured former CBS anchor Dan Rather saying that the network had made a mistake in hiring Couric because they wanted "to try to bring *The Today Show* ethos to the *Evening News*, and to dumb it down, tart it up, in hopes of attracting a younger audience." Tart it up, huh? Dumb it down? Wonder if he would have used those words if CBS had hired a man. Something tells me no.

Like so many of the other double standards, this one has more serious consequences than you would initially think. Young women who think that in order to be attractive they have to be dumb are deliberately not showing how smart they are or not spending nearly as much time developing their minds as they are developing their looks.

HeyUGLY.com and *CollegeBounds CB Teen* magazine did a survey to find out if young girls were pretending to be dumber than they actually were, for fear of scaring off boys: 35 percent of them admitted they were. Too depressing for words. But it's not exactly surprising. In a world that values young women for their looks and doesn't even believe that their smarts exist, it only makes sense that girls would work their hardest to look good over anything else. They're rewarded for looking a certain way. Being on the math team? Yeah, right.

# So... what to do?

Let's start rewarding girls for making smart choices and for being smart women. Make the math team cool again! (Okay, this may be wishful thinking on my part because I was, in fact, a math-team dork. Hi, Mr. Li!) Let's let young girls know that we can indeed look good *and* be smart. That we don't have to forgo our brains in order to impress. And for the love of god, let's please stop watching reality television. Please?!

# 38

# HE'S AN ACTIVIST,
## SHE'S A PAIN IN THE ASS

**MEN WHO ARE POLITICAL—WHETHER THEY BE ACTIVISTS,** organizers, or politicians—are passionate, driven, intellectual. Women activists, however, are big fat pains in the ass. They're neurotic and annoying—they're not taken seriously. Unfortunately, this is one double standard I know all too much about.

While men who work for change are revered and admired, women who do the same are often scoffed at, dismissed, or outright hated. And it's been happening for a long time.

Take women who fought for the right to vote. If you take a look at any of the political cartoons from back in the day, you'll find a lot of caricatures of suffragists as old, ugly ladies who are beating men up. Seriously. (Those feminist stereotypes have been around a while!) Another asks, "When women vote, who will wear the pants?" Unfortunately, the negative reaction to women's activism wasn't just op-eds and political cartoons. In a 1913 protest organized by women suffragists, women were literally attacked (so much for treating us like ladies and all!): People spat at the marching women, and mobbed and beat them. The police, who were supposed to protect the marchers, did nothing. Over two hundred protestors were injured. Women like Alice Paul and Lucy Burns, who were imprisoned for their protests several years later, were beaten in prison along with other suffragists. Their poor treatment came to light later, but it's not often talked about. (The movie *Iron Jawed Angels* is all about it; you should check it out.) Men who fought for such basic rights and put up with abuse are quoted throughout history books. We get a chapter, if we're lucky.

Later in feminist history, women activists were not so much outwardly abused as they were ignored. Because, you know, women couldn't possibly have anything interesting or important to say.

Susan Brownmiller, in the book *In Our Time,* tells of a pivotal moment, in the beginning of the second-wave women's movement, that occurred at the 1968 National Convention for New Politics. Jo Freeman and Shulamith Firestone had drafted a resolution on women, which was to be met with an all-too-familiar pooh-poohing:

> Back at the main session, Jo ran down the aisles handing out copies of the resolution while Shulie charged to the podium. "Cool down, little girl," the session chairman told her. "We have more important things to talk about than women's problems."

Brownmiller also discusses the reaction of her male counterparts after women marched in an anti-war demonstration with a float dedicated to women's rights: "The peace activists were appalled. . . . Stopping the Vietnam War was still the chief priority, wasn't it. . . . [This] action, they howled, was petty, disloyal, divisive."

Nice, huh?

I hate to say it, but women's voices in politics are treated much the same way today. When we bring up reproductive justice or racism, for example, we're focusing on "single-issue" politics.

A recent kerfuffle in the repro rights sphere happened when several (male) activists and writers suggested that we just forget about *Roe v. Wade*, the case that made abortion legal—because it was causing too much division. They argued that if we just left the abortion decision to the states, it would be all good. And what about the women in states where abortion was illegal? Too bad for them. So basically, the Daddy Dems wanted the little ladies to pipe down and let the men worry about what was best for them. (I find it interesting that when it comes to making concessions for the good of the party, women's rights always seem to be first to go.)

This isn't to say that all men in politics ignore women's voices. I'd like to think that we have more allies today than we ever have. Blogger Scott Lemieux, from *Lawyers, Guns, and Money*, weighed in on this particular controversy with considerable aplomb:

> Indeed, what is finally most intolerable about the new anti-*Roe* consensus is just this willingness to throw the rights of others under the bus while patting oneself on the back for making noble compromises. It is certainly easy for men living in blue state urban centers—who know that no woman in their family or social circle will ever be denied a safe abortion—to casually dismiss the importance of the rights of poor women in the two dozen states at high risk of banning or severely restricting access to abortion in a post-*Roe* world.

Other men, like Scott, speak out on behalf of women every day. But it kind of sucks that it takes a man speaking about these issues in order for people to take it seriously.

So... *what to do?*

Make our voices heard as often, and as loudly, as possible. If you're an activist, don't let men dominate the conversation—speak up!

# 39

# HE'S A PERSON,
## SHE'S A COMMODITY

**GUYS CAN BE WHOEVER THEY WANT TO BE.** They can be funny or shy. They can curse or be super-polite. And they can be complex human beings with developed personalities. Now, of course, women can do that, too. (Perhaps better?) But while we do all the things men do and have all of the feelings and personal characteristics that they have, we'll always be one thing they aren't: a commodity.

And I'm not just talking about prostitution or trafficking. I'm talking about the way that women's bodies are presented as objects every single fucking day, everywhere we go. You can't turn a street corner without seeing a woman being used to sell something (anything)—and really, what's being sold is her. It's us.

Okay, to be straight-up . . . "commodification" is one of those words that get thrown around a lot in women's studies class, so I'm almost loath to use it so frequently when discussing this double standard. But I think it's important. The way that women are turned into commercial objects—for people to buy and dispose of when they want—contributes to a culture that thinks it's okay to do violence to women. Because we're not really people, we're objects.

I knew that women were objectified in the media, in society, but I didn't realize the extent until I was in college and saw this amazing film, *Killing Us Softly*, by Jean Kilbourne. The movie juxtaposes advertising images—which are disturbing enough on their own—with images of violence against women who are objectified, dehumanized, and used to sell things. Soon, the images of violence and the ads are so intermingled that you really can't tell which is which. In the version I saw (Kilbourne changes the film from time to time to update the ads), the movie ended with the horrifying rape scene from the Jodie Foster flick *The Accused*. Because it all comes together—how ads, movies, and music videos all contribute to the idea that women are less than, that we're not real people, that it's okay to hurt us. It's very overwhelming.

And it's what makes people think it's okay to write articles like one that ran in *Forbes*, a respected publication, about the economics of prostitution. It started off like this: "Wife or whore? The choice is that simple." Nice, huh? Wait—it gets better.

> [The researchers] admit that spouses and streetwalkers aren't exactly alike. Wives, in truth, are superior to whores in the economist's sense of being a good whose consumption increases as income rises—like fine wine. [W]ives and whores are—if not exactly like Coke and Pepsi—something akin to champagne and beer.[1]

Women, wives, "whores" are like Coke or Pepsi, champagne and beer. Just let that sink in a minute. It doesn't hurt to know, however, that the reporter for this piece also penned an article about how men shouldn't marry "career women." So that gives you a little insight into where he's coming from!

Outside of ads and the way that women are talked about as if we're not real people, there are, of course, more obvious forms of commodifying women and women's bodies—like sex work. In this case, women's actual bodies are being bought and sold. While there are feminists who argue that it's not actually women's bodies but women's labor (sex) that's being bought, I think we'd all agree that prostitution *does* give men the impression that women are for sale. Which is horrible. (That isn't to say I'm against sex work—I'm not.)

Reproductively, we're also commodities. Women's eggs are bought and sold regularly, and a woman who wants to make some extra money can just be a surrogate—carry a baby for a woman who can afford to pay you. Of course, surrogates usually end up being low-income women or even women from other countries—way to commodify other women!

I think the most important thing to remember is that the United States relies on women's commodification. Whether the idea manifests itself in slapping an anorexic model, or airing a slinky ad for perfume, or visiting strip clubs, or white women "renting" uteruses from women of color in "third-world" countries, women's bodies are for sale.

# So... what to do?

Questions about sex work, porn, and the like have been mulled over by so many different feminists, it's hard to know where to begin. Same with women-as-objects and how our bodies are commercialized. Some folks think that this is where feminism begins and ends. All I know is that it pays to be hyperaware of it, to be critical of the ways you see women being presented, and to think about your choices and how they affect other women. At least it's a start.

# 40

# HE'S A PUBLIC FIGURE,
## SHE'S A VIRGIN/ WHORE

**HOW MANY ARTICLES DO WE HAVE TO READ ABOUT** Lindsay Lohan's cooter? Or Britney's relationships? Or Paris's sex tape? I'm done! I don't want to see or hear about one more article, blog post, television segment, or water-cooler chat about women celebrities and their sexual escapades. I just can't. Not until, that is, I start seeing the same kind of coverage for male celebrities and public figures.

I want a Denzel Washington sex tape. A Brad Pitt cock shot when he's getting out of a car. Gossip about what a whore and a shitty parent Kevin Federline is—okay, I get some of that already, but you see what I'm getting at.

Men who are in the public eye can get away with just *being*, without their sexuality being on display or talked about. Women celebrities, on the other hand, are made into virgins or whores by the public—which says a lot about what society thinks about women in general!

We start sexualizing our female celebs early. I mean, how many Mary Kate and Ashley jailbait jokes did you hear before they were "legal"? There was even a website dedicated to a countdown to the twins' eighteenth birthday! 'Cause there's nothing sexier than an underage girl, I guess. So long as she's a virgin.

Half the attraction to underage women celebs seems to be the idea that they're virginal. Think pre-disaster Britney Spears and pre-marriage Jessica Simpson. Same thing with the new media obsession with Hayden Panettiere, the seventeen-year-old star of the television show *Heroes*. (At a recent awards show, there were more jokes about her upcoming eighteenth birthday than anything else.) Though while we expect them to be virginal, we also expect them to appear as sexual as possible. Hypocrisy abounds!

Once these young women get older, get married, have babies—in other words, can no longer be seen as innocent and virginal—the public tears them to shreds, mocks them, and calls them fat old sluts. There's no winning.

What's particularly interesting to me is that feminism often takes the blame for this oversexualization in pop culture! Rather than blaming the society that demands this kind of impossible standard for women (be virginal but whorish), countless articles I've read conflate third-wave feminism with sexy pop culture. It's laughable.

The idea is supposedly that since feminism sought to make men and women equal, women are now acting like, and having sex like, men. (You know, because women weren't sexualized at all before feminism.) But the truth is, this new level of sexualization is just a modernized take on the virgin/whore complex. Where, of course, men get off easy.

And it's killing us. Look at the downfall of women like Britney Spears, so obviously in need of help, yet roundly mocked. It's time to end the insanity and start being compassionate. Blogger Courtney at A Feminist Response to Pop Culture writes of Spears:

I think that her body politic is extraordinarily problematic especially since she is simultaneously marketed to young girls as an idol and to men as a masturbatory fantasy. But note how I write that "she is marketed" as if she is no longer an independent entity but a piece of public property. Not long ago one of my friends and I got into a debate about whether Spears chose this life path. My friend argued that she deserves what is happening to her because she chose to become a part of the public domain. But remember, she was but a child when she made that choice and she hardly could have anticipated the hyper-sexualization and invasion that would come along with that "choice." Further, does anyone really deserve that kind of dehumanization?

I think we can agree—hell no, they don't.

# So... what to do?

As with anything to do with celebs and the media, it's difficult to make an impact. But we can make a stink to editors of magazines and newspapers who continue to perpetuate the idea that women should be forever sexualized. Or we can just wait for and dream of that Brad Pitt cock shot.

# 41

# ∮ HE'S GOT
# G.I. JOE,
## SHE'S GOT BARBIE

**MY FAVORITE SHOW WHEN I WAS A KID WAS *SHE-RA.*** My sister and I used to fight over who got to be the "princess of power." Like, physically. I think that little girls are always attracted to strong women and girl characters—probably because we're not given all that many to choose from. For me it was Anne of Green Gables and Ramona Quimby. Though it was a close call between them and Gem; I *so* wanted to be a rock star.

But as I got older, it seemed there were fewer and fewer female characters on television for me to identify with. (Which is probably part of the reason I spent so much time reading!) Men can choose any kind of character they want—they play everyone from CIA agents to doofy single guys trying to get the girl to cops to doctors.

But now, when I look at the TV that teen women are watching—I have to say, I'm even more depressed. The female characters are *eh*—not to mention that most of them are white. *Gossip Girl* and *The O.C.*; reality shows and ditzy women characters who want to shop more than anything else. . . . I mean, at least I had Buffy!

Without a doubt, *Buffy the Vampire Slayer* is probably one of the most feminist shows there is. Shit, women's studies departments even have small conferences on the show! There were fully developed, strong female protagonists; a main character was a lesbian; and the messages were undoubtedly about gender equality. I frigging *miss* Buffy.

Joss Whedon, creator of *Buffy* and the master of writing awesome female characters, gave this amazing speech at an event for feminist organization Equality Now about how odd it is that so many people asked him why he wrote so many great roles for women—as if there needs to be a reason:

> Why aren't you asking a hundred other guys why they don't write strong women characters? I believe that what I am doing should not be remarked upon, let alone honored, and there are other people doing it. But, seriously, this question is ridiculous and you just gotta stop ... because equality is not a concept. It's not something we should be striving for. It's a necessity.[1]

(And people actually wonder why women swoon over this guy?)

What's also interesting about the current state of TV (or movies, for that matter) and capable female characters is that a lot of the more badass women characters out there come from comic books. Like Elektra, or the women on the NBC show *Heroes*, which is supposed to be kind of a television-comic. Normally I'd have no issue with this—hell, I'll take good characters where I can get them!—but when you look at the actual comics ... ugh. Big breasts, small waists, overwhelmingly white—very standard, stereotypical male-fantasy stuff.

So where can we look today for our new Buffys?

Even beyond female characters, there's still a long way to go for feminism on television. Despite the fact that about 40 percent of

American women will have an abortion sometime in their lifetime, you won't see abortion portrayed on TV. (They may *talk* about abortion if a character gets pregnant, but she'll inevitably have a miscarriage and be grateful that she didn't have to make the decision. Convenient.) And when they do show something "controversial," it often spreads misinformation. On an episode of *Veronica Mars*, for example, the writers confuse the morning-after pill (which prevents pregnancy) with a medical abortion (a pill that ends a pregnancy). I've seen the same mistake on *Law & Order* as well.

And when it comes to queer characters or people of color, we're also doing pretty shitty. Unless you're watching shows that are *about* people of color or queer people—think *The L Word* or *The Parkers*—the norm is considered white and straight, and race and sexuality issues are rarely discussed. Don't you think we're a little beyond this shit? Though I must make a shout-out to *All My Children* (don't laugh—I used to watch with my grandma!), which not only featured the first lesbian character and kiss on daytime television, but also had a transgender character who wasn't a hooker or psycho—unfortunately, a first. The show even worked with trans organizations to make sure that it was portraying the character in an accurate (and respectful) way.

Clearly, we have a long way to go. While women are still being shown as vapid bimbos who would just like to shop all day, instead of as strong, complex, and *real* women, we're in trouble.

# So... what to do?

Don't watch or support shows that portray shitty women characters. And write letters to networks telling them you'd like to see stronger women on television. Thank networks when they get it right—maybe then we'd still have shows like Geena Davis's *Commander in Chief* and even a new chapter in my beloved *Buffy*. A girl can hope!

# 42

# HE'S PAYING LESS,
## SHE'S PAYING MORE

**SO, WE KNOW THAT WOMEN EARN SUBSTANTIALLY LESS MONEY** than men, so it would make sense that we pay less for products and service, right? No such luck. Women pay more for haircuts, dry cleaning, cars, even mortgages. Why? Well, for no other reason than that we're women. It's a little something I like to call the vagina tax.

You know why I like where I get my hair cut (Bumble and Bumble, represent!)? Because they don't split up prices by gender. But plenty of stylists do, despite the fact that hair length these days doesn't really have anything to do with a person's sex.

This may seem like splitting hairs (apologies for the bad pun), but the truth of it is, women are paying a lot more for consumer services than we should. In fact, a 1994 study found that gender-biased pricing cost California women more than $1,300 a year—and almost $15 billion annually (!) for all women. That's no chump change!

For example, a study out of Northwestern University found that white women paid more than $150 than white men for identical cars. And get this—black women paid $400 more than black men and $800 more than white men! A New York City study also showed that when women price used cars, 42 percent of dealers quote a higher price to

JESSICA VALENTI

women. Women also pay 20 percent more for haircuts and 25 percent more for laundering services.[1]

Frances Cerra Whittelsey, author of *Why Women Pay More: How to Avoid Marketplace Perils*, says, "I found that women truly do pay more—and get less." Whittelsey puts much of the blame on sexism: "Women pay more for haircuts and dry cleaning because of 'traditional' pricing.... Women pay more for auto repairs and used cars and new cars ... because the people who sell these services believe we are suckers and decided we are the ones on whom they can make their profit margins."

Nice, huh?

But the disparity doesn't stop at everyday, seemingly shallow costs like clothing and beauty needs. In 2007, *The New York Times* reported that despite women's having better credit scores than men, they pay more for mortgages:

> [A] study released last month by the Consumer Federation of America, a nonprofit advocacy group, [shows] that women are 32 percent more likely to carry mortgages with high-interest rates than men with similar incomes. And wealthier women were 50 percent more likely to carry expensive loans than their male counterparts.
>
> ... In 2005, according to the study, 10 percent of women who took out mortgages received the highest-cost subprime loans, compared with about 7.5 percent of men.[2]

Another study from Harvard Medical School researchers showed that women pay more for health coverage under high-deductible health insurance plans.[3] The study found that men spend less than $500 per year on medical deductibles, while women spend more than $1,200, and that only a third of men insured by a high-deductible plan spend over $1,050 per year in medical costs, while 55 percent of women do.

Steffie Woolhandler, lead author of the study, says, "High-deductible plans punish women for having breasts and uteruses and having babies. When an employer switches all his employees into a consumer-driven health plan, it's the same as giving all the women a $1,000 pay cut, on average, because women on average have $1,000 more in health costs than men." (This is because, like I mentioned in discussing the healthcare double standard, women need more pre-ventative care than men—like Pap smears, mammograms, birth control, and so on.)

Insane. Sexism is robbing us blind, ladies!

# So... what to do?

Thankfully, people are doing something about the vagina tax. (Sorry, I just love that name.) For example, California created the 1995 Gender-Tax Repeal Act, which makes it illegal to discriminate based on gender when it comes to the pricing of services. Similar legislation was passed in Florida's Miami-Dade County, New York City, Pennsylvania, and Massachusetts. And you can take action, too—if you see a gender-based pricing difference at your dry cleaner, hairstylist, or anywhere else, speak up. Bring it up in your community. Because while paying more for a haircut may not seem like the biggest deal in the world, it's adding up—and women just can't afford sexism everywhere in our lives!

# 43

# ♀ HE'S PUSSY WHIPPED,
## SHE'S A "GOOD GIRLFRIEND"

**WHY IS IT THAT WHEN A GUY DOES THINGS THAT ARE NICE** or considerate for the girl he's involved with, he's called "pussy whipped," but the same behavior is just expected from women? We're *supposed* to care (a lot) about what men think about us. Just take a gander at the cover of any women's magazine out there and you'll know what I mean: See what he thinks of your breasts! Does he really love you? When will he pop the question?! Ugh. When it comes to (straight) love, men are whipped, but women are . . . women.

Urban Dictionary defines "pussy whipped" as a "situation where-upon a male is undeniably at the mercy of his high-maintenance girl-friend & answers to her every beck and call, usually followed by the reprioritizing of girlfriend over friends, family, school, food, water, and air."[1] Replace that with "female" and "boyfriend" and tell me if it sounds odd. . . . Nope, it doesn't. Because that's what women are expected to do for their male partners every day. (Fun fact about "pussy whipped": Besides being a gross term, it's also the name of Bikini Kill's debut album. Love Kathleen Hanna. *Love*.)

From the time we're little girls we're taught that our end goal in life, basically, is to get a man. (Never mind if we're gay—find a man anyway!) From playing house as kids to devouring teen mags to becoming Bridezillas—our main focus is supposed to be relationships. And, by proxy, men. We're supposed to care what they think of the way we look, how we talk, walk, act. Frankly, it's fucking exhausting.

Not only does the excessive caring about what men think mean that women are more likely to undergo ridiculous amounts of work to "improve" the way we look—it also means that we don't always do what's best for us.

We may not speak out at work for fear of what someone will think of us. We may not speak up in a relationship, or during sex, because we've been taught to be accommodating. We may forgo job opportunities, travel opportunities, friendship opportunities—it's all just too much.

And frankly, it could be dangerous. There are scores of stories about women who ended up being assaulted because when a strange guy approached them, they were too afraid of being considered rude to tell him to fuck off. Or to listen to their instincts that said something was off. I remember a story we read in one of my first-ever women's studies classes, about a woman who was walking up to her apartment with groceries when a couple of things fell out of her hand. A man happened to be in her hallway and offered to help—he picked up the groceries and said, "Open the door; I'll carry them in for you." Despite being uncomfortable, she let him into her apartment because she didn't want him to think that she was rude or—get this—that he was some sort of rapist or something. He ended up attacking and raping her. Obviously, this is an extreme example, but I think it's worth noting that there can be scary consequences for being taught to be "nice" all the time.

Men, however, are actively taught that if they care *at all* what women think of them, they're some sort of softy, a "pussy." (Nothing worse than being a girl, remember?) My college boyfriend Mike—who was just this amazing person—was routinely mocked and criticized by his friends because he was nice to me. Just nice. He wasn't letting me walk all over him and he wasn't a saint—but just by being a pretty decent guy he was given shit and labeled "whipped."

This double standard not only makes day-to-day life kind of miserable, but it also reinforces gender norms—the idea that women should be the nice, accommodating ones and that men are supposed to be "tough" and not give a shit what their girlfriend, or any other woman, thinks.

Now, there may be gals out there who don't give a flying fuck what men, potential dates, whoever, think of you. Awesome. You rock. (I'd certainly like to think that I'm in that group of nonchalant ladies.) And I'm certainly not writing this in order to paint women as sad sacks who are overly concerned with other people. I bring it up because this is the shit that is shoved in our faces from the time we're kids. And like it or not, it's hard to avoid and even harder not to fall for. But we can try.

# So... what to do?

Stop obsessing about what other people (male *or* female, for that matter) think of you. It's a waste of time and energy. Stop buying magazines that presuppose your biggest concern in life is landing a man. Start doing things for yourself—stuff that makes you happy and successful, not anyone else. And of course, most important, have fun. (Which, trust me, is a lot easier to do when you're not forever worried about what a guy thinks.)

# HE'S PROTECTED, SHE'S PROPERTY

**WHETHER THEY'RE ABOUT ABORTION, RAPE, OR SOMETHING** more innocuous—like vibrators—there are rulings, laws, and legislation still around that embody double standards and hypocrisy. These are just a few.

*Rape* . . . One would hope that the days of blaming the victim and equivocating about what constitutes rape are long gone. But even now, thirty years after feminists fought to bring national attention to the rape epidemic, women are still faced with ridiculous qualifiers when it comes to "proving" sexual assault.

In 2006, a Maryland appellate court ruled that once a woman consents to sex, she can't change her mind. Not if it hurts, not if her partner has become violent, not if she simply wants to stop. You may be scratching your heads right now—after all, who would continue to have sex with an unwilling partner *besides* a rapist? It doesn't take a genius to know that no *always* means no—no matter when it's said. But it seems that reason and rationality have no place in Maryland.

Or take the nineteen-year-old Howard University student who, after being drugged and sodomized, was denied treatment at local hospitals because she "appeared intoxicated"—not so surprising, given the nature of her attack. Even when the teen went to police for help, she

JESSICA VALENTI

was outright dismissed. Sergeant Ronald Reid of the MPD Sex Assault Unit has been quoted as saying, "[I]f we don't have reason to believe a crime happened, we wouldn't administer a rape kit." Apparently, intoxicated women can't be assaulted.

One of my favorites: A judge in Nebraska banned the word "rape"—at a rape trial. The victim couldn't even say "assault." The only word she was allowed to say at the trial of the alleged attacker? "Sex." The judge argued that using the word "rape" would be too prejudicial. Shockingly, at robbery trials no one is banned from using the word "mugging." (Thankfully, the victim was having none of it: "I refuse to call it sex, or any other word that I'm supposed to say, encouraged to say, on the stand, because to me that's committing perjury. What happened to me was rape; it was not sex.")

Another woman in Massachusetts was told she wasn't really raped—she was defrauded. She went to bed one night, in the bedroom she shared with her boyfriend, when a guy she thought was her boyfriend got into her bed and had sex with her. Turns out it was her boyfriend's brother pretending to be her lover. But somehow, that's not rape. The court said that Massachusetts law defines rape as intercourse "by force and against [the] will" of the victim and that "fraudulently obtaining consent to sexual intercourse does not constitute rape as defined in our statute."

Did you know that if you are raped while you are sedated, you don't need to know? A ruling in Oregon came down saying that rape victims who are unaware they were raped shouldn't be informed. (This case comes from the trial of a doctor who assaulted women when they were out of it right before surgery.)

*Pay* . . . There's plenty of discrimination when it comes to pay equity, but I had to mention this one because it was a Supreme Court decision. The court's ruling in *Ledbetter v. Goodyear* says that employees must make their discrimination complaints within 180 days "after the alleged unlawful employment practice occurred." So if a woman doesn't realize that she's being paid less than her male coworkers within 180 days, too bad.

*Fun* . . . Vibrators are still illegal to buy and sell in eight states. While these seem like they would be old laws, just last year an Alabama court upheld the ban on vibrators, saying the law wasn't unconstitutional because selling sex toys is like "prostitution." (With yourself?!)

*Life* . . . A town in Missouri bans people from living together who aren't related by "blood, marriage, or adoption." So no cohabiting for all you sinners! The law received attention after a couple was denied an occupancy permit in the town because the woman's partner wasn't the father of one of her three children. Charming.

*Violence* . . . An Ohio man who beat up his girlfriend had his conviction voided because he wasn't married to her—the ruling said that domestic violence can happen only within marriages. So if the girlfriend wanted to press charges? She'd have to marry her abuser.

Now, I could go on and on—there are laws on the books and rulings out there that you wouldn't believe. I really just wanted to bring these up to highlight how fucked up things still are on so many levels. And how much work we still have to do.

# So... what to do?

I don't know, dude. Move?

# 45

# ♀ HE'S FONDLING,
## SHE'S FEEDING

**I LIKE MY BOOBS, ALWAYS HAVE.** While plenty of less-than-polite comments have been levied against the girls over the years (especially since I started blogging, wow), I continue to hold my ta-tas in high esteem. And though the idea of a baby having its way with them doesn't exactly fill me with eager anticipation, I've resigned myself to the idea that that's what they're there for—so all will be well when I do have a kid.

The boob double standard doesn't involve a male equivalent so much as it does men's viewpoint that breasts belong to *them,* are there for them to look at, ogle, suck on, what have you. So when you do anything that reminds guys what breasts are really for—you know, like feeding babies—they get all ornery. Problem is, when you *don't* breastfeed, you're accused of not being a good mom. So you can't win either way.

I hate to be the one to say it . . . but I will. Boobs are not for boys. Sure, guys, you can get them on loan—but they don't belong to you. They belong to us. You can make as many boobie-related novelty products as you want (blogger Shakespeare's Sister found over 150—including boobie shampoo dispensers and pencil erasers!), and you can slap a fake pair on every lad-mag cover you want. It doesn't change the basic fact that boobs are future baby food.

One of my fave boobie moments—because it was the most telling—came from political commentator Bill Maher, who went on a tirade against public breastfeeding. In discussing a protest that women held after a breastfeeding mother was kicked out of a restaurant, Maher went off. He fell back on some predictable quips ("They say it's natural—so is masturbating, but I generally don't do that at Applebee's!"), but it was the jokes-that-aren't-jokes that were truly insulting: "Look, there's no principle at work here other than being too lazy to either plan ahead or cover up.... It's not fighting for a right, it's fighting for the spotlight."

Now, I don't have a kid, so when I wrote about this on Feministing, I relied on Kelly Mills at baby blog Babble to take him down:

> There he totally hit the nail on the head, didn't he? I mean, I had no desire to actually get out of the house or anything when I ate in restaurants; I just wanted a little attention. In fact, that's why I chose to feed my baby with my exposed tits in the first place. I mean, yes, it's recommended by every doctor ever and it's good for the kid, but of course that was secondary to my desire to have total strangers jump in my face and say, "Good job on the procreation!" Why, I know that when I walked into restaurants people looked thrilled to see me and my infant, and I'd hoist her onto my shoulders, whip out my boobs, and say, "Gimme some sugar, folks!"[1]

Amazing. Another boobs-for-boys-only jerk was columnist Rabbi Shmuley Boteach, who gave advice to married women not to breastfeed in front of their husbands (lest the men be turned off by lactating):

> The erotic nature of a wife's body is one of the principal ele-
> ments of attraction in marriage. When a husband ceases to
> see his wife as a woman, and begins to see her as "the mother
> of his children," a negative trend has begun in his mind that
> can only subvert his erotic interest.[2]

Right, 'cause who would want to fuck the mother of his children? Grody. I have a feeling *this* is what's at work with Maher, Rabbi Boteach, and a lot of other men who take issue with public breastfeeding. They resent that a woman's public body—her exposed or partially exposed breast—could be there for someone other than them, for something other than sexual consumption. After all, if a woman is exposed in public, it's supposed to be because she's flashing her tits for beads or taking money in a G-string—not for feeding babies. That's not sexually arousing, and therefore it's unacceptable.

But god forbid a woman *doesn't* breastfeed her kids—then she's a bad mother! A lot of mothers have a difficult time breastfeeding—it can be a painful and long process. (So I hear.) But in the day of super-mom syndrome, whipping out the formula instead of the titty can seem like a failure. Especially in a society that demands so much of mothers: Breastfeed, but don't do it in public and offend onlooking men!

# So... what to do?

This is a hard one. It's not like we're ever going to convince straight guys to stop talking about or looking at our titties. But I think groups that call themselves "lactivists" have the right attitude. They're fighting all across the United States to make sure that women have the right to breast-feed in public, and they're spreading information about breastfeeding as well. Also, never forget that no matter how many advertisements, magazine covers, or assholes make you feel like the girls are some sort of public commodity—they're not.

# 46

# ♀ HE'S CHILDLESS,
## SHE'S SELFISH

**SINGLE MOMS IN THE UNITED STATES ARE PORTRAYED** as a blight on society—selfish, irresponsible women who aren't doing the right thing by their kids. (And by "right thing," of course, we mean being married.) Single dads, however, are heroes—men who are victims of an irresponsible mother who left, or perhaps widowers; they're men who have picked up the slack and done the impossible . . . a woman's job.

In 2005, nearly 1.5 million babies were born to unmarried women, with women in their twenties accounting for a good portion of them. The National Center for Health Statistics reported that 35.7 percent of all births were to unmarried women—55 percent of the births for mothers in their early twenties were to unmarried women; for women in their late twenties it was almost 28 percent.[1] Those are pretty big numbers. (Though the study didn't take into account whether or not the women were cohabiting with partners, or what their sexuality was.)

As someone who was never really sure about getting married, but absolutely sure about having kids, I have to say that I've considered single motherhood. (Though I figure I have another few years before I start worrying about it, despite all the scare tactics telling me that my eggs are *dying* by the minute.) While I'd rather have a partner, I also would like

JESSICA VALENTI

to be a younger mom. So what's holding me back? I can admit it—the stigma against single mothers scares me.

We already know that there's a double standard when it comes to parenting, but when we're talking about single parenting, the judgment is even harsher.

Take Louise Sloan, for example. Author of *Knock Yourself Up: A Tell-All Guide to Becoming a Single Mom*, Sloan tells her own story of getting pregnant via artificial insemination when she was forty-one years old, as well as the stories of other single gals.

After Salon.com ran an interview with her, the vitriol she got in the Letters section was horrible.

> [T]he boy will be screwed up or resent women, not having had a father around. he will have a higher chance of being a criminal. he will likely understand that all the feminist piffle shoved in his head is the opposite of what men need to know to be EFFECTIVE and happy free agents in the bigger world.
>
> Your child will grow up fatherless and disadvantaged. But you got what you want, and that is what is most important. How sad.

And those are just a couple; there were a ton more letters calling Sloan selfish and saying that her son will grow up to be dysfunctional. There's just something about a single mom by choice that really pisses people off. So . . . predictable.

Sloan gets off a lot easier, though, than single mothers of color. Woo, boy, does the American public ever love to hate single moms who aren't white. They must be welfare queens or irresponsible moms who pop kids out by the dozen. There is no end to the racism/classism/sexism matrix here!

That's why single moms also get hit with the work conundrum. While we hear all of this media frenzy about women opting out of the workforce to become stay-at-home moms, single moms *have* to work. While the rate of women working outside the home has pretty much leveled off for most groups of women, it's actually jumped for single mothers—from 63 percent to 75 percent. Single moms are also more likely to be in poverty.

But for all the shit that single moms take—people love single dads! I think I've seen three Lifetime movies in the last month about heroic single dads who take care of their kids after a shitty mom leaves. (Uh, not that I watch Lifetime at all . . . I swear.) Not. Fair.

# So... what to do?

Have your families the way you want—and don't let anyone give you shit for it. And if you hear people spreading anti–single mom myths, call them out on it.

# 47

# ♀ HE'S FUNNY,
## SHE'S ANNOYING

**IF I HEAR ONE MORE PERSON SAY WOMEN AREN'T FUNNY,** I may just lose it. Because, fuck you, *I'm* funny. And also, you know, because of the sexism.

When men tell jokes, they're funny. Women comedians? Annoying wenches, it seems. Why is it that women comedians get the shit end of the stick so often? Or that women in general are just assumed to be the comedically challenged gender?

The most controversial (and asinine) article to come out recently on women and humor was by Christopher Hitchens in the January 2007 issue of *Vanity Fair*. The oh-so-charming title? "Why Women Aren't Funny." The headline pretty much says it all, but there's more. Hitchens' basic argument was that women aren't funny because they don't *have* to be. Men, he says, try to be funny to get women to like them. Women have sex appeal to attract the opposite sex, so there's no real reason for them to be funny. In addition (and this beats all), apparently women aren't funny because we have the babies:

> For women, reproduction is, if not the only thing, certainly the main thing. Apart from giving them a very different attitude to filth and embarrassment, it also imbues them with the kind of seriousness and solemnity at which men can only goggle.[1]

See, and here I thought stuff coming out of vaginas was supposed to be hilarious. Thank goodness I have someone like Hitchens to set my feeble female mind straight. But it's not just douches like Hitchens who are perpetuating the women-aren't-funny myth. Canadian psychologist Eric Bressler did research on humor and claims that "women want a man who is a humor 'generator,' while men seek a humor 'appreciator.'"[2] Meaning we're supposed to laugh at guys' jokes but not tell any ourselves. Another researcher mentioned in the same article goes even further. Don Nilsen, a linguistics professor at Arizona State University and a self-proclaimed expert on humor, says that men are turned off by funny women: "I think every man in the world loves the humor, even the sexual put-down humor, of Judy Tenuta or Joan Rivers. . . . But very few men want to marry them." I'll be sure to tell my boyfriend, who laughs his ass off at my jokes, that he's actually mistaken. He doesn't like me at all. Actually, the best response to this "science" was from blogger Melissa McEwan, better known as Shakespeare's Sister: "To which men, exactly, is that sense of humor a turnoff? Oh, yeah—the kind of men no woman with a wicked sense of humor gives a diddly shit about."[3] Exactly.

Female comedians aren't taking this only-men-are-funny nonsense sitting down. Janeane Garofalo (who I met once and was sooo nice) has said, "Funny transcends gender. . . . The best comics regardless of gender are more detail oriented, good social critics, and can laugh at themselves. And hacks are unfunny in the same way."[4] But while funny may transcend gender, people aren't always comfortable with humor *about* gender. Julia Sweeney, who played the gender-ambiguous Pat on *Saturday Night Live*, was quoted as saying that on the show women "were almost accused of having a victim 'agenda' if they brought out scenes that addressed sexism." Ick. Oh, and the best comedian response to Hitchens that I've seen? Writer Jill Soloway and a group of her comedian friends started having "Fuck Christopher Hitchens" events featuring bands, booze, and all sorts of funny women. So there.

If it were only the stereotype that was being perpetuated, I might be able to deal. But funny women are feared—and mocked—all too often for me to not say anything about it. Think about the vitriol that Roseanne Barr, Ellen DeGeneres, and Rosie O'Donnell—all successful funny ladies—get. These comedians get called "ugly" on the regs, but what I find most interesting is that they're often called "grating" or "annoying." Kind of relates to the idea that women shouldn't be loud—funny women are breaking with tradition, so people (men) find them intimidating. Let's face it, funny is powerful. (Just another reason people love to call feminists "humorless." Little do they know!) In an article on women and humor on AlterNet, reporter Emily Wilson interviews stand-up comic Beck Krefting, whose dissertation at the University of Maryland was about women and comedy: "It's okay for guys to crack jokes and be the class clown, but if a girl did it, she was marked the strange one.... That was true in elementary school and high school and then on the stage."[5]

## So... what to do?

Be funny. Encourage your hilarious friends to go and try some stand-up comedy. And for the love of all things feminist, don't date anyone who thinks funny women are a "turnoff." Okay, just one date—but only if you go wearing a clown nose or throw a pie in his face or something.

Oh, and for good measure, here's my favorite joke of the moment: What do parsley and pubic hair have in common? You push them both to the side before you eat.

# ♦ HE'S DATING, SHE'S TAKEN

**WHEN I WAS IN HIGH SCHOOL,** I had a boyfriend who was a tad possessive. He would get jealous if I spoke to other guys—because I was "his"—and for Valentine's Day he got me the oh-so-thoughtful gift of a beeper, so he could get in touch with me constantly. Keeping tabs is *très* romantic, didn't you know? I bring this up not to make you all cringe with embarrassment for me (though you should—I sported that ugly-ass beeper every day for a year), but because it's just a small example of how women are marked as "taken."

Whether we're attached or not—single, dating, engaged, married—straight women are subject to a ton more qualifiers than men when it comes to sharing our relationship status.

*The ring* . . . Nothing says ownership like a brand-spanking-new, über-expensive engagement ring! I've written about engagement rings before on Feministing and in *Full Frontal Feminism*—I mean, how could I not?—but it seems that there's always something new to talk about when it comes to rings. They're the ultimate mark of a taken woman—and something that men aren't expected to wear in return. (Why not just pee on her to mark your territory? I say. Some gals are into it.) Meghan O'Rourke of *Slate* doesn't pull any punches when it comes to the all-controversial ring:

# 48

But there's a powerful case to be made that in an age of equitable marriage the engagement ring is an outmoded commodity—*starting with the obvious fact that only the woman gets one* [emphasis mine]. The diamond ring is the site of retrograde fantasies about gender roles.[1]

It's always been the consumerism behind engagement rings that bothers me most. As if you can't really be in love without spending a substantial sum of cash. I guess it's just always struck me as . . . well, unromantic. But as O'Rourke points out, there is something just wrong about the fact that only a woman is visibly marked as engaged. It reeks of a "Woman mine!" caveman mentality, but we've romanticized it to the hilt.

(This isn't to say I'm against rings altogether. When my friend Lauryn got engaged, her boy bought her this amazing art deco sapphire ring that he spent forever looking for, and he made a little book about the ring's history and how he came to find it. It was from the heart, not the wallet. Though perhaps she should have gotten him something to mark his ass as taken, too!)

*Miss, Ms., Mrs., oh my!* . . . Once we've gotten married (that is, for those of us it's legal for), we have the privilege of three honorifics, rather than just the one that males get. You would think the more choices the better, but all these prefixes do is force women into deciding how much we want people to know about our marital status. It's just gross. Men's titles have absolutely *nothing* to do with whether or not they're hitched, yet we have to come clean? Of course, we do have the lovely "Ms.," thanks to '70s feminism that found it ridiculous that women should have to reveal their marital status within their name. I definitely use it—not just because of the sexist connotations of the other choices, but because "Miss" makes me think of an eight-year-old, and "Mrs." makes me think of all the bitch teachers I had. (Who the hell else do you call "Mrs. So-and-so"?) Of course, "Ms." doesn't come without its problems as well. Whenever I've corrected someone and asked them to call me *Ms.* Valenti, I've gotten the *Oh, you're one of those* look or some sort of jokey/snide comment. It's a real pain in the ass.

*His last name* . . . We've already gone over this nonsense, but I just wanted to remind folks—just one more way we're marked as taken and he gets off with, well, his actual name. Lucky him.

*Puppy love* . . . I'm not sure how pervasive this trend is—but these T-shirts that preteens and teens are wearing saying shit like "I love my boyfriend" and such irritate me. Perhaps I'm being picky, but it strikes me as odd and somewhat controlling.

*The unmarked single woman* . . . Ah, how nice it is to be unencumbered by rings, names, and dumb shirts. Though I think all you single gals out there know what I'm talking about when I say that I'm kind of sick and tired of people assuming that because I'm single they have the right to ask me all sorts of relationship questions. *Why* are you single? *When* are you getting married? Ugh. Can't a gal just enjoy her alone, unmarked time?

# So... what to do?

I say, stay mum on your relationship status when it comes to physical markings like rings and titles. But that's just me. It just seems ridiculous that women should have to brand themselves according to whether they're attached, while men can do whatever they want without anyone giving it a second thought. Though perhaps now, in the age of Facebook and MySpace, where everyone can publicly display their relationship status with "single," "dating," "married," "in a relationship," or the ever-dreaded "it's complicated," there will be some sort of relationship-marking equality. (Though I still resent finding out about an ex's new relationship via Facebook feed. Harsh.)

# 49 HE'S RUGGED, SHE'S RUDE

**IF YOU'VE EVER READ MY WRITING BEFORE,** then you know I have a bit of a potty mouth. Okay, I fucking curse. A lot. Between being raised Italian and being raised in Queens, I never stood a chance! Also, I must admit, my manners were never all that fantastic. I was the awkward girl who was always being told to sit up straight, stop talking with my mouth full, and for god's sake stop running around with skinned knees through my dirty stockings. (Hey, I was a tomboy, but I liked me some tights!) I wasn't so annoyed as a kid by the idea that I should act a little less nuts—but I was constantly irked that my male peers weren't told the same thing. You know, because boys will be boys and all that jazz.

Anything less than prim, "ladylike" behavior from women is considered rude, yet for men it's just pure testosterone and manliness. I call bullshit. Why is it that etiquette really refers only to women? (Politeness for boys is more about chivalry than anything else—which, as we know, is pretty mired in sexism itself!)

Not that etiquette handbooks are super popular anymore with younger women, but the sheer number of guides and manuals on how to be a proper "lady" is staggering. Seriously, just check out Amazon and type in "etiquette"—you'll be shocked. Now comes my disclaimer: I'm not advocating rude behavior or saying that being polite is anti-feminist. I'd like to think that I'm a courteous person (a loud, opinionated, courteous person, but still). But the way that we define "rude" when it comes to women seems more than a little problematic to me—it requires that we're more quiet than we need to be, more accommodating than we need to be, and less of ourselves than we should be.

For example, it seems like way too much advice aimed at women is of the "suck it up" variety. Take Slate's advice column, "Dear Prudence." In 2005, Prudence got a letter from a woman who was constantly having to clean up after her boyfriend and was "burned out being the only one to clean the house." Prudie's advice? Just deal.

> It is sometimes easier to pick up the guy's socks than to make continual "requests." Given that he is slothful and chaotic around the house (and may also have retro ideas about men and women), it might be easier on you to bear in mind what a great guy you have while you pick up his socks.[1]

See, ladies, if you just think happy thoughts (whistle while you work!) while you pick up after your man, it's a lot "easier." Ugh.

What's also particularly annoying to me about the politeness double standard is that it's just steeped in racism and classism. When I was mocked for my Queens accent in my Manhattan school, or when I saw my girlfriends of color get chastised for being too "loud," I knew that it wasn't just about decorum. It's about an image of ideal womanhood that's not only quiet and subservient—but also white and upper class.

There's also a sexual aspect to politeness that should make all women uncomfortable. In much the same way that the virgin/whore complex creates "nice" girls or "naughty" girls, etiquette as it is now sees sexuality as, well . . . rude! When I did an article about the "modesty movement" in 2006—basically a regressive group of gals who'd like to see women back in the home and forever virginal—the connection was clear.

> One site sells the ModesTee, a black leotard meant to be worn underneath less "appropriate" clothing. It is touted as "a fashionable solution to dressing modestly by turning the clothes that may be a little too sheer, too short, or too low into clothes you can wear." Another company, WholesomeWear, sells modest swimwear. This layered—yes, layered—swimsuit is made up of spandex and nylon and covers most of the body. A bit like a waterproof kaftan. . . . But being modest does not end at your wardrobe. Alexandra Foley, a thirty-four-year-old mother of four who blogs at Modestly Yours, says: "Modesty is both your outward appearance and your interior disposition. A woman can be modestly dressed, but not carry herself in a modest way."

Get that? The way you dress reveals what your "interior disposition" is. 'Cause short skirts are just . . . rude. So what is this really about? Why is it so important that women act "polite"? Because if a docile, quiet woman is the ideal, that means we can be shamed for speaking up. There's a reason feminists are often called "too loud" or "rude"—it's a silencing strategy.

# So... what to do?

Be as loud as you want to be. (I certainly am.) Be courteous, be nice, be polite—but do it in a way that doesn't infringe on the person you are. And if people tell you that you're too opinionated or not "ladylike" enough, tell them to go fuck themselves.

#  HE'S PLAIN, SHE'S VAIN

**FOR A SOCIETY THAT TELLS WOMEN** that in order to be beautiful we have to be tanned, plucked, waxed, sucked, and primped, we sure do like making fun of the gals who live up to the ideal! While the male model of rugged, manly roughness is rarely mocked (hell, we put him on Brawny paper towels!), women who meet the feminine ideal are most often made fun of, called stupid and shallow, and dismissed as vain. It seems there's no winning for pretty girls, either!

Men who are beautiful are revered. Sure, you'll occasionally see the dumb-jock stereotype or the hot but vapid model—but that's nothing compared to the disdain that we heap upon gorgeous women. The hypocrisy is, if women *don't* take steps to be "beautiful"—whether it be through a weekly manicure or something more drastic, like plastic surgery—then we're slobs. But if we do, then we're vain.

It's something similar to the celeb-hate we love so much, but worse—because we do it to each other every day as well. Be honest— how often do we see a woman with a fake tan, or dyed hair, or obvious plastic surgery, and judge her—even if it's just a little? Don't feel too bad; we're trained to do as much. We're supposed to simultaneously want to be that woman—and want to destroy her. (And maybe hate ourselves for wanting to be her.) It's all sorts of fucked up. But it drives the competitive spirit that keeps women buying more products, more surgeries, more everything. A lot of people are depending on our judging and hating each other!

Another sad fact is that feminists aren't immune to the woman-hate. Oh, how I wish we were. Unfortunately, I've heard way too many feminists get down on a gal because she wore heels or lipstick—saying she was a pawn for the beauty industry or fooling herself. The thing is, this kind of faux "concern" isn't much different from what society wants us to do to each other—tear each other down, judge, and not get anywhere against the folks who are really hurting women.

Like the media. Reality shows are a subject unto themselves, but I think that they represent a tremendous example of how we punish women for conforming to the very expectations that we shove down their throats. If you want to know anything and everything about feminism, sexism, and reality television, you need to read Jennifer Pozner. She's like the feminist Queen Bee of reality TV. In an article she wrote for *Ms.* magazine, she discusses how the producers of this nonsense break women down:

> Viewers may be drawn to reality TV by a sort of cinematic schadenfreude, but they continue to tune in because these shows frame their narratives in ways that both reflect and reinforce deeply ingrained societal biases about women, men, love, beauty, class, and race. The genre teaches us that women categorically "are" certain things—for example, no matter their age, they're "hot girls," not self-aware or intelligent adults.[1]

You can find similar nonsense in almost all of the reality shows. They thrive on presenting us with hot, made-up women and then making them look as silly and pathetic as possible.

Gossip magazines also make a career out of shaming women who conform. On one page of a celebrity weekly you'll find close-up pictures of a star's cellulite, mocking her. But on the very next page, you're likely to see an article about how horrible and anorexic another woman star is. How often do we see spreads on male stars' fat asses? Or their dramatic weight loss? Not so often. Much more fun to shame women.

# So... what to do?

Stop hating. Seriously. Women have a hard enough time without other women giving us shit. And the truth is, we all do what we have to in order to get by in a society that hates women. For some of us, it's high heels and makeup. For others, it's plastic surgery. I don't think any of it is *good* for women, but I don't think judgment is particularly helpful either. Now, some of you may not want to hear this, but here goes: Don't buy magazines that do this to women. I know the celeb mags are popular, I do. But take a step back and look at what they're doing to women. Look at what they're telling you about women. Is that really something you want to be a part of? (Besides, if you want fashion and celebrity news, there are plenty of blogs and sites you can go to that don't rely on shaming.)

# NOTES

## ❷ HE'S CHILL, SHE'S ON THE PILL

1. Chaker, Ann Marie. "College Students Face Rising Birth-Control Prices," *Wall Street Journal,* July 26, 2007.

## ❸ HE'S ROUGH, SHE'S DAINTY

1. www.creditcards.com/credit-card-news/young-women-suffer-from-greater-debt.php.

## ❺ HE'S METROSEXUAL, SHE'S ANOREXIC

1. www.kaisernetwork.org/daily_reports/rep_index.cfm.

## ❼ HE'S A BACHELOR, SHE'S A SPINSTER

1. Mapes, Diane, ed. *Single State of the Union: Single Women Speak Out on Life, Love, and the Pursuit of Happiness.* Emeryville, CA: Seal Press, 2007.

2. Angier, Natalie. "Men. Are Women Better Off With Them, or Without Them?" *New York Times,* June 21, 1998.

## ❿ HE'S GONNA BE A SUCCESS, SHE'S GONNA BE A STAY-AT-HOME MOM

1. www.sciencedaily.com/releases/2007/10/071015102856.htm.

## ⓫ HE'S A POLITICIAN, SHE'S A FASHION PLATE

1. Aday, Sean, and James Devitt. "Style Over Substance: Newspaper Coverage of Female Candidates. Spotlight on Elizabeth Dole." The White House Project, 2000.

2. www.thewhitehouseproject.org/newsroom.

3. Alvarez, Lizette. "Speaking Chic to Power," *New York Times,* January 18, 2007.

4. http://feministing.com/archives/006376.html.

5. http://feministing.com/archives/006061.html.

6. Givhan, Robin. "Hillary Clinton's Tentative Dip into New Neckline Territory," *Washington Post,* July 20, 2007.

## ⓰ HE'S MANLY, SHE'S SASQUATCH

1. Winterman, Denise. "Letting your hair down," BBC News, January 12, 2007.

### 19 HE'S THE BOSS, SHE'S A BITCH

1. Johnson, Tory. "Why Doesn't the Devil Wear Brooks Bros.?" ABC News, July 3, 2006.
2. www.msnbc.msn.com.

### 20 HE'S WELL PAID, SHE'S SCREWED

1. American Association of University Women, "Behind the Pay Gap," 2007.
2. Interview with Sara Laschever, August 24, 2007. Feministing.com, http://feministing.com/archives/007616.html.
3. Vedantam, Shankar. "Salary, Gender and the Social Cost of Haggling," *Washington Post*, July 30, 2007.

### 22 HE'S HIMSELF, SHE'S MRS. HIMSELF

1. Friess, Steve. "More men taking wives' last names," *USA Today*, March 20, 2007.

### 23 HE'S GETTING AN EDUCATION, SHE'S GETTING IN HIS WAY

1. "More women graduate. Why?" *USA Today*, May 29, 2006.
2. Rosser, Phyllis. "Too Many Women in College?" *Ms.* magazine, fall 2005.
3. Jan, Tracy. "Schoolboy's bias suit," *Boston Globe*, January 26, 2006.
4. Pollitt, Katha. "Girls Against Boys?" *The Nation*, January 12, 2006.
5. Mathews, Jay. "Study Casts Doubt On the 'Boy Crisis,'" *Washington Post*, June 26, 2006, A01.
6. Rosser, Phyllis. "Too Many Women in College?" *Ms.* magazine, fall 2005.

### 24 HE'S INDEPENDENT, SHE'S PATHETIC

1. Roberts, Sam. "51% of Women Are Now Living Without Spouse," *New York Times*, January 16, 2007.

### 25 HE'S A CELEB, SHE'S A MESS

1. Traister, Rebecca. "Hit her, baby, one more time," *Salon*, September 12, 2007, www.salon.com.
2. Harris, Paul. "Bad girls oust wild men as the sinful darlings of Hollywood scandal sheets," *Guardian*, July 29, 2007.

### 26 HE'S HUSKY, SHE'S INVISIBLE

1. Meltzer, Marisa. "Are fat suits the new blackface?" *bitch: feminist response to pop culture*, Winter 2001.
2. http://kateharding.net/2007.

### 27 HE'S A MAN, SHE'S A MOM

1. www.npr.org/templates/story/story.php?storyId=12513004.
2. www.local6.com/family.
3. www.healthscout.com/news/1/609234.

### 28 HE'S DATING A YOUNGER WOMAN, SHE'S A COUGAR

1. www.thisisby.us/index.
2. www.urbandictionary.com.

### 29 HE'S DRUNK, SHE'S A VICTIM

1. www.alternet.org/story/48835.

### 32 HE'S REPRESENTED, SHE'S A TOKEN

1. www.ipu.org/wmn-e/classif.htm.

### 33 HE'S NEAT, SHE'S NEUROTIC

1. www.umich.edu/news.
2. www.angryharry.com/eshousework.htm.
3. www.washingtonpost.com/wp-dyn.
4. http://feministing.com/archives/008007.html.
5. http://news.bbc.co.uk.

### 34 HE'S FUN, SHE'S FRIVOLOUS

1. www.debbieschlussel.com/archives/2007/11.

### 35 HE WALKS FREELY, SHE GETS HARASSED

1. Valenti, Jessica. "Is segregation the only answer to sexual harassment?" *Guardian*, August 3, 2007.

### 39 HE'S A PERSON, SHE'S A COMMODITY

1. www.forbes.com/entrepreneurs.

### 40 HE'S A PUBLIC FIGURE, SHE'S A VIRGIN/WHORE

1. http://afeministresponsetopopculture.blogspot.com.

### 41 HE'S GOT G.I. JOE, SHE'S GOT BARBIE

1. www.americanrhetoric.com/speeches/josswhedonequalitynow.htm.

## 42 HE'S PAYING LESS, SHE'S PAYING MORE

1. Whittelsey, Frances Cerra. "Why Women Pay More," The Center for Responsive Law, 1993. Found online at www.holysmoke.org.
2. "Mortgages; Why Women Pay Higher Interest," *New York Times*, January 21, 2007.
3. Associated Press, "Popular health-insurance plans punish women," April 6, 2007.

## 43 HE'S PUSSY WHIPPED, SHE'S A "GOOD GIRLFRIEND"

1. www.urbandictionary.com.

## 45 HE'S FONDLING, SHE'S FEEDING

1. www.babble.com/CS/blogs.
2. Boteach, Shmuley. "Moms, Don't Forget to Feed Your Marriages," www.beliefnet.com.

## 46 HE'S CHILDLESS, SHE'S SELFISH

1. www.usatoday.com/news/health.

## 47 HE'S FUNNY, SHE'S ANNOYING

1. www.vanityfair.com/culture.
2. www.psychologytoday.com/articles.
3. http://shakespearessister.blogspot.com/2005/10/women-arent-funny.html.
4. www.msmagazine.com/summer2004/womenshumor.asp.
5. www.alternet.org/story/61102.

## 48 HE'S DATING, SHE'S TAKEN

1. www.slate.com/id/2167870.

## 49 HE'S RUGGED, SHE'S RUDE

1. www.slate.com/id/2119985.

## 50 HE'S PLAIN, SHE'S VAIN

1. www.msmagazine.com/fall2004/unrealworld.asp.

# ACKNOWLEDGMENTS

**FIRST AND FOREMOST,** thank you to my mother, father, and sister Vanessa for being forever supportive. You all mean everything to me. Thanks to my agent, Tracy Brown, for his advice and warmth, and to my editor, Brooke Warner, for her saintlike patience and for always believing in the work. Big thanks also go to Gwen Beetham, Ann Friedman, Jen Moseley, Samhita Mukhopadhyay, Celina De Leon, and Courtney Martin—my partners in feminist crime. Soon, ladies, we will take over the world. And last, thanks to Andrew Golis, for everything.

# ABOUT THE AUTHOR

© Adam Joseph

**JESSICA VALENTI** is the founder and executive editor of Feministing.com and the author of *Full Frontal Feminism: A Young Woman's Guide to Why Feminism Matters*. She has a master's degree in women's and gender studies from Rutgers University and has worked with national and international women's organizations. Jessica is also a cofounder of the REAL hot 100, a campaign that aims to change the perception of younger women in the media, and the blogger for NARAL Pro-Choice America. Her writing has appeared in *Ms.* magazine, *Bitch*, AlterNet, *Salon, Guernica* magazine, and the *Guardian* (U.K.), as well as the anthologies *We Don't Need Another Wave* and *Single State of the Union*. In 2007, she received a Choice USA Generation award for her commitment to reproductive-rights issues and was named one of *ELLE* magazine's 2007 IntELLEgentsia. She lives in her hometown of Astoria, Queens, with Neidra the cat, Monty the dog, and Andrew the boyfriend.

# SELECTED TITLES FROM SEAL PRESS

*Full Frontal Feminism* by Jessica Valenti. $15.95, 1-58005-201-0. A sassy and in-your-face look at contemporary feminism for women of all ages.

*It's a Jungle Out There: The Feminist Survival Guide to Politically Inhospitable Environments* by Amanda Marcotte. $13.95, 1-58005-226-6. All the witty comebacks, in-your-face retorts, and priceless advice women need to survive in politically hostile environments.

*30-Second Seduction: How Advertisers Lure Women Through Flattery, Flirtation, and Manipulation* by Andrea Gardner. $14.95, 1-58005-212-6. *Marketplace* reporter Andrea Gardner focuses on the many ways that advertising targets women, and how those ads affect decisions, purchases, and everyday life.

*She's Such a Geek: Women Write About Science, Technology, and Other Nerdy Stuff* edited by Annalee Newitz and Charlie Anders. $14.95, 1-58005-190-1. From comic books and gaming to science fiction and blogging, nerdy women have their say in this witty collection that takes on the "boys only" clubs and celebrates a woman's geek spirit.

*Abortion Under Attack: Women on the Challenges Facing Choice* edited by Krista Jacob, foreword by Rebecca Walker, afterword by Gloria Feldt. $15.95, 1-58005-185-5. This book is a call to action, in this conservative time, for new and veteran pro-choice people alike.

*Body Outlaws: Rewriting the Rules of Beauty and Body Image* edited by Ophira Edut, foreword by Rebecca Walker. $15.95, 1-58005-108-1. Filled with honesty and humor, this groundbreaking anthology offers stories by women who have chosen to ignore, subvert, or redefine the dominant beauty standard in order to feel at home in their bodies.